The Wholly Book of Doo-Doo-Rot-on-Me

The Wholly Book of Doo-Doo-Rot-on-Me

By
Jay Dubya

www.bookstandpublishing.com

Published by
Bookstand Publishing
Morgan Hill, CA 95037
4243_1

ISBN 978-1-63498-066-1

Printed in the United States of America

Other Books by Jay Dubya

Adult Fiction
Black Leather and Blue Denim, A '50s Novel
The Great Teen Fruit War, A 1960' Novel
Frat' Brats, A '60s Novel
Ron Coyote, Man of La Mangia
So Ya' Wanna' Be A Teacher
Pieces of Eight
Pieces of Eight, Part II
Pieces of Eight, Part III
Pieces of Eight, Part IV
The Wholly Book of Genesis
The Wholly Book of Exodus
Nine New Novellas
Nine New Novellas, Part II
Nine New Novellas, Part III
Nine New Novellas, Part IV
Fractured Frazzled Folk Fables & Fairy Farces
FFFF&FF, Part II
Mauled Maimed Mangled Mutilated Mythology
Thirteen Sick Tasteless Classics
Thirteen Sick Tasteless Classics, Part II
Thirteen Sick Tasteless Classics, Part III
Thirteen Sick Tasteless Classics, Part IV
Prime-Time Crime Time
UFO: Utterly Fantastic Occurrences
Time Travel Tales
Suite 16
One Baker's Dozen
Two Baker's Dozen
Snake Eyes and Boxcars
Snake Eyes and Boxcars, Part II
Shakespeare: Slammed Smeared Savaged & Slaughtered
Shakespeare: S, S, S and S, Part II
Poe: Pelted Pounded Pummeled and Pulverized
Twain: Tattered Trounced Tortured and Traumatized

Young Adult Fantasy Novels and Stories
Pot of Gold
Enchanta
Space Bugs, Earth Invasion

Contents

Background

On April 1, 2002 Mohammed Kareem Jihad, a fourteen-year-old April Fool Palestinian revolutionary, was ascending a rocky ledge along rugged cliffs that bordered the western banks of the *Dead Sea*. Exhausted from his climbing enterprise, young Jihad stopped to rest his weary body. The vernal radical lit a *Camel* cigarette and surveyed the arid landscape below. Much to his frustration everything seemed calm and serene.

When Mohammed Kareem Jihad leaned backwards his gaunt frame slipped through a narrow crevice between two limestone crags. The disoriented youth rose to his knees, inspected his shadowy surroundings and soon realized that he had fallen into a cave (containing a remarkable ancient artifact). In the center of the small hollow was an urn, a well-preserved remnant from Hebrew antiquity.

Instead of sticking his hand into the urn to feel for any contents Mohammed followed his dreadful terroristic instincts by pulling the pin of a hand grenade and tossing the explosive device into what was surely a great archeological discovery. When the bomb exploded prematurely, Mohammed Kareem Jihad had not yet fully exited the cave. Besides shrapnel, two leather objects bound with straps (strapnel) had blasted out of the ancient urn and collided with the back of the Palestinian lad's skull, knocking him unconscious.

When Mohammed Kareem Jihad finally regained his faculties *(his rich uncle owned two radical Arab universities),* he perceptively noticed and then grabbed the leather pouches and fled the scene of destruction. After descending the perilous cliffs the young militant thought, 'I'll bet whatever is inside these two leather packages is worth at least a carton of cigarettes,' so the youth mounted his stolen desert "quad" and motored to the city of Jericho, where his economically struggling father owned a popular café.

Inside the café Professor Phillip Collins of the Semitic Semantic Institute was seated at a table with Dr. Allen Qaeda from the Arab Aramaic Academy. Mohammed Kareem Jihad rushed into the dismal café and approached the cozy round table where the two distinguished scholars were conversing.

"How much will you give me for these two leather pouches?" the boy anxiously asked Professor Al Qaeda. "I need to buy some weapons right away!"

"Let's unravel them and see what ya' got!" the suddenly curious researcher replied. The good academic doctor gently unwound the dusty cords that bound the leather wrappings. Inside both packages Dr. Allen Qaeda discovered dozens of remarkably well-preserved papyrus sheets with ancient writings carelessly scribbled upon the archaic scrolls.

"Why it's the first two books of the Old Testament!" Professor Al Qaeda exclaimed in astonishment, "*The Book of Genesis* and *The Book of Exodus!*"

Professor Phil Collins, who knew plenty about Genesis, rendered his authoritative impressions. "This translation has much more detail than the presently read first two books of the Old Testament!" the Biblical expert enthusiastically observed and shared. "This type of papyrus dates back to at least 900 BC, which makes it a lot older than the Dead Sea Scrolls that had been re-written by the Essenes during an ancient creative writing class."

"If this historical account is accurate," interrupted Professor Al Qaeda, "then this great discovery will present a *wholly* new perspective to religious history, which is presently very controversial to begin with."

Young Mohammed Kareem Jihad was growing very impatient with the scholarly adults' intellectual evaluation and speculation concerning *his* fabulous find. "How much are they worth?" he insisted on knowing. "I need new weapons now!"

"Two cartons of American cigarettes, definitely!" Professor Phil Collins promised.

"And we'll even throw in an AK-47 and two slightly used hand grenades," Dr. Al Qaeda added.

"Sold!" an elated Mohammed Kareem Jihad gleefully shouted. "Now I can blow up my' younger sister's doll collection and her Jewish friends too!"

And so, Dr. Al Qaeda and my uncle Professor Phil Collins (on my mother's side of the family) became the legitimate owners of the only authentic "First Two Books of the Wholly Bible." The two eminent researchers believed that the remainder of the "unabridged" Old Testament had been thoroughly obliterated inside the urn when Mohammed Kareem Jihad's hand grenade had quite effectively exploded.

Fortunately Uncle Phil Collins had made a computer file in English of his meticulous translation of the great archeological treasure. Uncle Phil very thoughtfully and confidentially had electronically sent "Wholly Genesis" and "Wholly Exodus" to me as essential e-mail attachments. The careful deciphering represented my relative's fantastic interpretation of the ancient Hebrew writing, which I had electronically received on April 10, 2002. Regrettably, on April 11th, Uncle Phil and Dr. Al Qaeda were blown to smithereens by an errant Palestinian rocket while refining their study of the ancient scrolls in Professor Collins' Jerusalem home. The papyrus sheets and the original computer file had also been destroyed in the malicious terrorist attack.

My treasured e-mail translations are the only remaining evidence of *The Wholly Book of Genesis* and *The Wholly Book of Exodus.* Uncle Phil sincerely believed that the versions presently in my possession were the original and most reliable documentation of the "Word of Moses," who was believed to be the organizer of the popular *Genesis* and *Exodus* renditions that appear in the standard *Bible.* Uncle Phil Collins and Professor Al Qaeda strongly believed that Moses had fabricated the Biblical Genesis and Exodus stories around 1400 BC. But since writing (and bona fide alphabets) did not appear until the time after Homer and King David, around 1,000 BC, the Biblical stories had been handed-down and distorted because of the common practice of oral tradition with storytellers adding and subtracting important details for four prehistoric centuries.

Uncle Phil Collins and Dr. Al Qaeda professed that young Mohammed Kareem Jihad's accidental discovery represented the true unabridged stories of *Genesis* and of *Exodus.* They maintained that the new versions are much more valid in scope and content since the accounts had been written hundreds of years earlier than the stories that now appear in the first two books of the *Bible.* Thus, Mohammed's find is closer to Moses' language and intent than later popularly read interpretations of *Genesis* and *Exodus.* "Careless Hebrew historians and ancient priests recklessly modified the *Wholly Genesis* and *Wholly Exodus* versions into more pious, moral and self-righteous texts," Uncle Phil academically stated in his final e-mail letter. "The arrogant fools did it to satisfy their own selfish purposes and agendas."

Uncle Phil' also indicated in his e-mail, "Moses, who lived approximately 1450 BC around the time of Pharaoh Thutmose III of Egypt, didn't know how to write, even though he had put the stories of *Genesis* and *Exodus* together much like Homer had done with the *Iliad* and the *Odyssey.* In fact nobody knew how to write with any rhetorical expression skills until almost half a millennium later." According to Uncle Phil, "Moses barely knew the numerals one to ten signifying the *Ten Commandments* etched upon the famous twin stone tablets," my mother's older brother attested.

For a full decade after 2002, I had believed that only *The Wholly Book of Genesis* and *The Wholly Book of Exodus* existed in the treasured computer e-mail file, since a long blank void had appeared thereafter. But last month out of sheer boredom I ran the file to its end and remarkably discovered the fifth book of the Old Testament *Pentateuch, The Wholly Book of Doo-Doo-Rot-on-Me.* Apparently, *book* three *titled The Wholly Book of Numbers* along with book four, *The Wholly Book of Leviticus,* had somehow been accidentally erased in the e-mailed computer file.

Now that the essential background of *The Wholly Book of Genesis and The Wholly Book of Exodus* (along with the tampered-with computer file) is fully known, only the astute readers can be the best judges of the merits of Mohammed Kareem Jihad's remarkable discovery and of deceased Uncle Phil Collins' exceptional Biblical claims.

I have thoughtfully placed in *italics* the language that ancient scholars had shrewdly edited-out of the *Wholly Book of Doo-Doo-Rot-on-Me,* and I have plainly and clearly left the standard and generally accepted Biblical script in *Times New Roman* type.

Jay Dubya

Chapter One

"Historical Review and Exhortation"

The fifth book of the Pentateuch is called *The Wholly Book of Doo-Doo-Rot-on-Me, meaning "I feel full of shit after reading this utterly ludicrous fecal matter!"*

Exodus had described the rapid departure of the Israelites *(Jacob's people and clan)* from Egypt, continuing the nightmare adventures of the *Lord's* ill-starred "chosen people" *(cursed and punished Hebrews), and the rather absurd text begins* where the *Wholly Book of Genesis* leaves off.

Exodus recounts the oppression by the Egyptians of Jacob's descendants and their miraculous deliverance by God through Moses,' *(how they all filtered through Moses remains a huge mystery to this day), who then guilefully guided the Israelites out of Egypt without even the aid of a compass, a fortune teller or a crudely-drawn primitive map.*

Moses led the Israelites through the Red Sea *(which was really knee-deep shallow and blue)* to *famous* Mount Sinai *where nasty sinus infections were often cured by sneezing into a wicked gusty wind with real gusto from atop the desolate mountain's peak.* There, Moses entered into a special covenant with the Lord where God 'laid down the law' for all *the doltish Hebrews* to *faithfully* obey His *Original Formula* Ten Commandments *(Demandments). Hence, the landmark saying came into existence "to lay down the law," which when accurately translated into colloquial English means "to read the riot act without a lot of added bullshit."*

The Wholly Book of Doo-Doo-Rot-on-Me is a repetition of what passed at Sinai and Cadesbarne: and of the people's *constant crybaby* murmuring and their *well-deserved* punishment. *It is a basic repetition of Exodus because not only does history repeat itself, but coincidentally, Biblical History does also.*

$$* * * * * * * * * * * *$$

These are the *ridiculous* words, which Moses spoke to all Israel *(since his booming hoarse voice carried for hundreds of miles)* beyond the Jordan Torrent, in the plain wilderness, over against the Red Sea, between Pharan, *Fahrenheit* and Thophel, and Laban, *and Labia,* and Haseroth, where there is very much gold *and even a nifty pagan bull made out of bullion.*

1

Eleven days' journey from Horeb by the way of Mount Seir to Cadesbarne in the fortieth *(who gives a shit?)* year, the eleventh month, the first day of the month, *the eighth hour along with the fifth second of tedious travail,* Moses spoke to the children of Israel *(excluding the adults and the adulterers)* all that the Lord had commanded him to say to them: *"Go to the Promised Land that now belongs to other impostors!"*

After that *bullshit session of Moses addressing the apathetic Israelites,* he had slain Sehon, King of the *debaucherous* Amorrhites, *who had made love and had straight, lesbian and homo' sex morning, noon, and night,* and who dwelt in Hesebon *Cinnebon:* and *next the nomadic Israelites butchered* Og, the wizard king of the Basan *Basin,* who abode in Astaroth, and in Edrai, *not too far from the notorious Wizard of Og himself.*

Beyond the Jordan in the land of Moab *Dickie,* Moses began to expound the law, *and to unconvincingly say to his abundant disinterested and apathetic followers:*
"The Lord our God spoke to us in Horeb, *but only I had heard Him speak* saying: 'You have stayed long enough in this mountain: *how did you fools ever get into the actual active volcano without getting your chubby buttocks scorched and singed?* Turn you, and come to the mountain of the *pleasure-seeking* Amorrhites, and to the other places that are next to it, *of which I can't remember their particular names,* the *plain* plains and the *hillbilly* hills and the *myriad* vales towards the south, and by the sea shore, the land of the Canaanites, and of Libanus, as far as the great river Euphrates, *you loathsome lowlife fraidy cats'."*

"Behold, said he *(Moses or the Lord?),* although *I have no land deed or title, don't worry about the Demandment 'Thou Shall Not Steal'.* I have delivered it to you, *even without a functioning viable Post Office or competent Postmaster:* go in and possess it, concerning which the Lord swore to your *three un-biological* fathers Abraham, Isaac, and Jacob, that He would give it to them, and to their *plenteous sperm and egg* seed after them."

And I said to you at that time: I alone am not able to bear you, *either polar or grizzly:* for the Lord your God hath multiplied you, and you are this day as the stars of Heaven, for a multitude *of multiple multiplying purposes. It's also okay to practice addition, but*

2

it's evil to engage in subtraction and division when the Lord needs more mindless worshipers. (*Knowing mathematics in multiplying to the third power,* He, Lord God of your fathers, added to this *elusive* number many thousands, and bless you as He hath spoken *solely to me, Moses.*)

I alone am not able to bear your *(Israelites)* business, *which is none of my damned business anyway,* and the charge of you and your differences, *for I have other major things on my (Moses) busy pea-brain mind and on my empty pea-less plate.*

Let me have from among you wise and understanding men, *for I am basically chauvinistic when it comes to women,* and such whose conversations *and diatribes* are approved among your tribes, that I may appoint them *(only the men)* your *undisputed* rulers *and yardsticks.*

Then you *obnoxious knuckleheads* answered me: "The thing is good which thou meanest to do, *but exactly what the heck is it again? Repeat your stupid-assed bullshit Moses!*"

And I took out of your tribes men wise and honorable, and appointed them rulers, *tribunes, and centurions,* and officers over fifties, and over tens, who might teach you *pathetic dimwits* all things, *even ridiculous nonsense that I had never ever before imagined.*

And I *(Moses)* commanded them, saying: "Hear them, and judge that which is just: whether he be one of your country, or a stranger, *or an illegal alien, or a legal alien from another fucked-up nightmare planet.*"

There shall be no difference of persons, you shall hear the little as well as the great, *which I now recognize this zany statement as having more socialism than capitalism:* neither shall you respect any man's person *or personals,* because it is the judgment of God. And if any thing seems hard to you, *excluding your flaccid and limp reproductive organs,* refer it to me, *Moses,* and I will hear it, *see it, smell it, taste it, or if necessary, feel it with all ten arthritic fingers.*

And *also on my laundry list* I *(Moses)* commanded you all things that you were to do. And *after* departing from *the hoary whores* of

3

Horeb, we passed through the terrible and vast wilderness, which you' then saw, by the way of the *diabolical* mountain of the *sex-starved* Amorrhites, as the Lord our God had commanded us. And when we were coming into *the barns near* Cadesbarne, I said to you: "You are coming to the mountain of the Amorrhite, which the Lord our God will give to us. *We'll lay siege when the vile adulterers are indulgently having all kinds of normal and abnormal perverted sex.*"

See the *desolate barren* land which the Lord thy God giveth thee: go up and possess it, *even without money or gold or rare geld to barter.* As the Lord our God hath spoken to thy fathers: "Fear not, nor be any way discouraged *from pilfering either land or property from these crude inferior savages that doesn't belong to you.*"

And you came all to me, and said *all at the same time like a chorus of hilarious silly hyenas:* "Let us send men *that are not blind* who may view the land, and bring us word what way we shall go up, and to what cities, *ghettos, slums and barrios* we shall go *and conquer.* And because the saying *I had mentioned* pleased me *and me alone,* I *(Moses)* sent of you twelve men, one of every *fucked-up* tribe: Who, when they had set forward and had gone up to the *rugged-but-not-carpeted* mountains, *and eventually climbed to a new clime,* the *jerk-offs* came as far as the valley of the cluster: and having viewed the land, *all of them shit their already cruddy robes.*"

Taking of the fruits thereof *without the owners' unneeded permission,* to show its fertility, they *(the selected scout raiders)* brought them to us, and said *like Cretan cretins:* "The land *we soon will purloin and pillage* is good, which the Lord our God will *merrily* give us."

And you *incompetent worthless freaks-of-nature* would not go-up, but being incredulous to the *infallible* word of the Lord our God, you *gutless cowardly feckless Israelites* murmured in your tents, and said, *all of you preposterous parrots chattering at the same time:* "The Lord hateth us, and therefore He hath brought us out of the land of Egypt, that He might deliver us into the hand of the *amorous* Amorrhite, and destroy us *after* a *very few of our rank ranks lose our friggin' virginity and the rest of us lustful assholes decide to abandon our disgusting and frustrating sexual abstinence.*"

Whither shall we go up the *Mountain of Sin seeking amorous activity with the affectionate Amorrhites?* The messengers have *further tremendously* terrified our hearts, *testicles, tits and smelly assholes,* saying: "The multitude is very great, and *the pagans* taller than we, *since they have more protein and nutrition in their ample diets than we do:* the cities are great, and walled up to the sky, *where they have amazing cloud technology;* we have seen the sons of the Enacims there. *Apparently the Enacims and the neighboring Anacins have no daughters, prostitutes, sisters or wives: they just have giant-sized neurotic sons. Yes,* walled-up to the *friggin'* sky. *This is a* figurative expression, signifying the walls to be very high *and that to the Amorrhites and the women-less Enacims, 'the friggin' sky's the limit'.*"

And I *(Moses)* said to you: "Fear not, neither be ye afraid of them: *The bigger the bastards are, the harder they fuckin' fall!* The Lord God, Who is your *Fearless* Leader, Himself will fight for you, as He did in Egypt in the sight of all, *at least that is what I Sphinx and me alone saw.*"

And in the *wild* wilderness (as thou hast seen) the Lord thy God hath carried thee, as a man is wont to carry his little son, all the way that you have come, until you came to this *seemingly forsaken shithole* place. *Yes, I carried all one plus million' of you simultaneously!* And yet for all this *fantastic effort,* you did not believe the Lord your God Who went before you in the way, and *impressively* marked-out the place *without the use of any futuristic GPS devices,* wherein you should pitch your tents *and pitch your baseballs,* in the night showing you the way by fire, and in the day by the pillar of a cloud, *using my very own cloud technology recently obtained from Heaven's science.*

And when the Lord had heard the voice of your *silly sophomoric* words *coming from your parched throats,* He was angry and swore *without a Bible,* and *indignantly* said: "Not one of the men of this wicked generation shall see the good land, which I promised with an oath to your *three* fathers, *all of whom were big oafs to begin with.*"

Except Caleb, the son of Jephone *and Mega Phone:* for he shall see it *(newly acquired stolen territory),* and to him I will give the land that he hath trodden upon, and to his *delirious obnoxious* children, because he hath followed the Lord, *just like a mindless*

5

sheep follows a shepherd. Neither is His *(the angry Lord)* indignation against the people to be wondered at, since the Lord was angry with me (Moses) also on your *unworthy* account, and *the Boss nastily* said *to me:* "Neither shalt thou go in thither. *You Moses are a craven ineffective dolt, just like the screwed-up Israelites!"*

But Josue the son of Nun, thy minister, *that mother-less mother who had left the convent before becoming a Mother Superior,* he shall go in for thee *to pinch hit:* exhort and encourage him, and he shall divide the land *and its people* by lot to Israel. Your *deranged* children, of whom you said that they should be led away as captives, and your *nincompoop* sons who know not this day the difference of good and evil *or even the definite distinction between noon from midnight,* they shall go in: and to them I will give the valuable *pagan desert* land, *free of charge,* and they shall possess it, *and I won't even charge them admission or issue them any special tickets to enter the barren wasteland.* But return you and go into the wilderness by the way of the Red Sea, *which I have shrewdly dyed blue to fool all of you ninny simpletons along with thy pursuing Egyptian enemies riding advanced-technology chariots.*

And you answered me *all in unison because you have no individual brains inside your fucked-up diminutive craniums:* "We have sinned against the Lord: we will go up the mountain and fight *against the bigger sinners,* as the Lord our God hath *sternly* commanded. And when you went ready armed unto the *formidable* mountain, the Lord *exclusively* said to me *(Moses):* "Say to them, *the low-mentality imbeciles, morons and idiots:* 'Go not up, and fight not, for I am not with you: lest you fall before your *powerful sinful* enemies'."

I *emphatically* spoke, and you hearkened not: but resisting the *explicit* Commandment of the Lord, and swelling with *false* pride, *which was not too swell,* you *thick-headed nutcases* went up into the mountain *to join the extremely egregious Amorrhites who are always thinking with their (and your) reproductive organs and not with their (and your) brains in perpetually and indiscriminately committing adulterous sin.*

And the *abominable* Amorrhites that dwelt in the *distant* mountains coming out, and *maliciously* meeting you, *swarmed* and chased you, as *agitated* bees *would instinctively do: they did not beehive themselves* and made *instant* slaughter of you from Seir as far as Horma, *all the way to Hormona and Harmonica.* And when you *itinerant hapless weasels* returned and wept before the Lord, He heard you not, *and* neither would He yield to your *apologetic* voices, *for you dumb dunce-oriented assholes had miserably failed in your sacred mission.* So you *haplessly* abode in Cadesbarne *barns and stables* for a long time, *just to think, to plan, to connive and to masturbate.*

Chapter Two

"Northward along Edom"

They *(we)* are forbidden to fight against the Edomites, Moabites, and Ammonites *and also the dreaded Men-in-Knights' armor.* Their victory over Sehon king of Hesebon *Cinnebon was totally meaningless.* And departing from thence we came into the *wild, wild* wilderness that leadeth to the Red Sea, *not too far from the Dead Sea,* as the Lord had spoken to me *(Moses):* and we compassed Mount Seir a long time *and made a lot of noise using surround sound.* And the Lord said to me *and to me alone in that I was the only human who would listen to Him or who could ever hear Him:* "You have compassed this mountain *without a compass* long enough: go toward the north *arid wasteland* and command thou the people, *saying to the myriad imbeciles:* "You shall pass by the borders of your brethren the children of Esau, who dwell in Seir *near the infamous see-saws, and they will be afraid of you because I saw Esau sitting by the see-saw."* Take ye then good heed that you stir *not soup nor trouble* against them. For I will not give you of their land so much as the step of one foot, *yard or furlong* can tread upon, because I have given Mount Seir to Esau, for a possession, *just like his now non-functional dilapidated see-saw.* You shall buy meats of them for money and shall eat *before the carnage:* you shall draw *well* waters for money, and shall drink, *but endeavor to drink well water instead of sick water."*

The Lord thy God hath blessed thee in every work of thy hands: the Lord thy God dwelling with thee, knoweth thy journey, how thou hast passed through this great wilderness, for forty years, and thou hast wanted nothing *for four decadent decades except food, shelter, clothing, love, war and peace.* And when we had passed by our brethren *who never noticed the millions of us crawling, our non-perceptive brethren, being* the *non-perceptive* children of Esau, that dwelt in Seir, by the way of the plain from Elath and from Asiongaber *for you avid geography buffs to savor, relish, and muster, in order to catch-up,* we came to the way that leadeth to the *deserted* desert of *Moab Dickie, the very desert that obdurate Moab Dickie had never deserted.*

And the Lord said to me: *"Moses, invent an alphabet and learn how to write so that you can jot this incredible incredulous irrelevant stuff down, A-to-Z.* Fight not against the Moabites, neither go to battle against them, *for they might in due time become our tag-team partners:* for I will not give thee any of their land, because I have given Ar to the *lackadaisical lazy* children of Lot in possession," *whatever the hell that authoritative nomenclature from His lips means.*

The Emims, *without needing any towel-headed Imams,* first were the inhabitants thereof, a people great, and strong, and so tall that like the race of the Enacims, *were sort of like those dreadful Titans prevalent over there in Ancient Greece.* They *(the Emims)* were esteemed as giants, *like those other giants in the distant future in cities like New York and San Francisco,* and were like the sons *and sons of bitches* of the Enacims. But the Moabites call them Emims, *even though they have a few Rabbis and not many Imams among their various fucked-up clans.*

And Moses (me) said to my people: The Horrhites *(whose ugly horny women have sex without wanting to be paid for being laid)* also formerly dwelt in Seir: who being driven-out and destroyed, *for certainly it can't be the other way around,* the *fifty thousand homeless* children of Esau dwelt there, as Israel did in the land of his *(Esau's)* demon possession, which the *arbitrary* Lord *generously* gave *the pathetic bastard for free.* Then rising-up to pass the Torrent Zared, we came to it, *and believe me, it was absolutely torrential. Even our famished and thirsty cattle died from drowning, and we had to have surf and turf to eat, even the gay vegetarians and vain vegans among us.*

And the time that we journeyed *from the filthy fucked-up barns at* Cadesbarne till we passed over the *torrential* Torrent Zared, was thirty-eight *frustrating* years, *and most of us had drowned just like our famished thirsty cattle had done:* until all the generation of the men that were fit-*to-be-tied,* for war was consumed out of the *rebellious* camp, *camp counselors included,* as the Lord had sworn, *solely to me:* For His hand was against them, that they *the instigators* should perish from the midst of the camp. *Yes, the vindictive Lord was so mighty that He needed to use only one fist during the entire camp campaign.* And after all the fighting men were dead, *they were no longer fighting amongst us, and the deceased assholes couldn't say or do anything ever again.*

But the Lord spoke to me *(Moses)*, saying: "Thou shalt pass *like fecal matter* this day the borders of Moab *Dickie*, the city named Ar, *which is south of the border beneath what the bizarre low-intelligence locals call Grande River:* And when thou comest nigh the frontiers of the children of Ammon, *who was believed to be infertile, just like his deserted desert, and most important, impotent too,* take heed thou fight not against them, nor once *or twice* move to battle: for I will not give thee of the land of the children of Ammon, because I have given *a lot of it* to the children of Lot *in exchange* for a *lucky lotto* possession."

It was accounted *for,* a land of *colossal* giants: and giants *with giant appetites* formerly dwelt in it, whom the Ammonites call *Zombie* Zomzommims, a *vampire empire* people great and many, and of tall stature *as the enormous men in circus side-shows often are, just* like the Enacims whom the *bellicose* Lord destroyed *their enemas* before their face, *the whole tribe having only one face:* and He made them to dwell in their stead *and on their humble homesteads too,* just because He wanted to do so, *and for no other friggin' omnipotent reason other than simply, Holy Might Makes Holy Right.*

As He had done in favor of the numerous children of *sperm-less* Esau, that dwell in Seir, destroying the Horrhites *and their myriad hoary whores,* and delivering their land *via Hebrew Parcel Post* to them, which they *proudly* possess *without too many demons haunting there* to this day.

The *hostile* Hevites also, that dwelt in Haserim *as far away as the extremely sinful Gaza strip joints and bountiful Gaza burlesque and pussy parlors,* were expelled by the Cappadocians: who came out of *a large volcanic crater called* Cappadocia, and destroyed them and dwelt in their stead and on their *(the heavy fat Hevites) ramshackle stone and mortar* homesteads *and their fully decrepit brick and mortar stone store stalls.*

Arise ye, *said the insomniac Lord,* and pass the Torrent Arnon *and this time be sure to use flotation devices to prevent another mass drowning:* Behold I have delivered into thy hand Sehon, King of Hesebon *Cinnebon,* the Amorrhite, and begin thou to possess his *useless* land and make *additional* war against him, *because war, like greed, is good, and especially good for us contentious covetous invading Israelites.*

This day will I begin to send the dread and fear of thee *(Moses, you weak old wimp)* upon the nations that dwell under the whole Heaven, *the neatest celestial place where I happen to both live and reign all by My glorious lonesome Self: Yes Moses, the sky's the limit!* That when they *(the Un-United Nations)* hear thy name, they may fear and tremble *like apprehensive palsy victims,* and *they will* be in pain like *traveling pregnant* women in *tedious* travail, *all about to deliver sextuplets.*

So I *(obedient and hallucinating Moses)* sent *irresponsible* messengers from the *terrible* wilderness of Cademoth to Sehon, the King of Hesebon *Cinnebon,* with peaceable words, saying: "We will pass through thy land; we will go along by the *un-paved dirt* highway: we will not turn aside neither to the right hand nor to the left, *so don't expect any radical turn of events from us hallucinating Hebrew assholes.*"

Sell us meat for money, *make that 'meat for credit' because we have no cash to speak of,* that we may eat, *drink, screw and be merry with our wine, women and women harlots, for most of us are not gay or bisexual:* give us water for money and so we will drink *beer, swallow-down ample fire water and then gulping gallons of malt liquor.* We only ask that thou wilt let us pass through, *so act like you're a freakin' fake filter of sorts.*

As the children of Esau have done, that dwell in Seir, and the Moabites, *who take only small bites of food* and that abide in Ar, *not far from the fanatical maniacs in Ar-mania:* until we come to the Jordan, *not a future basketball player but a friggin' abandoned place,* and pass to the land which the Lord our God will give us *without any deed or title. We'll simply follow formidable archangels Gabriel and Michael into Jordan.*

And Sehon, the King of Hesebon *Cinnebon,* would not let us pass: because the Lord thy God had hardened his spirit *along with his extraordinary penis,* and fixed his heart *that was never broken, fractured or ruptured in the first damned place,* that he might be delivered into thy *(Hebrew)* hands *and coconut palms,* as now thou seest and *comprehendeth.*

Hardened, etc... That is, in punishment of his *(Sehon)* past *alleged* sins, *which cannot be described in either part' or in detail here for the sake of Biblical brevity.* He *(the Lord)* left him *(Sehon)* to his own stubborn and perverse disposition, *because Sehon was born with a stubbed-head,* which *artistically* drew him to *experience* his *ultimate* ruin.

And the Lord *confidentially* said to me (Moses): "Behold I have begun to deliver unto thee Sehon and his *worthless arid* land; begin to possess it *without the threat of evil spirits or demons."* And *then* Sehon came out to meet *and greet* us *along* with all his people, *both straight and fagged-out gay shit-heads, but mostly LBTG idiots, ready* to fight at Jasa.

And the Lord our God delivered him *(Sehon; a definite pronoun/antecedent problem demonstrated here)* to us: and we slew him along with *the whole slew of* his *clueless biological and non-biological foster* sons and all his *slew of expendable gender-problem* people *too.*

And we took all his cities at that time, killing the *peculiar* inhabitants of them, men and women and children *along with dogs, cats and also numerous pet crocodiles.* We left nothing of them, *and by the word nothing, I mean 'no-thing':* Except the *grazing* cattle, which came *un-grazed* to the share of them that took them: and the spoils of the *demolished* cities, which we *avariciously* took *un-spoiled, of course.*

From Aroer, which is upon the bank of the Torrent Arnon, *the bank where the natives kept their filthy gold and muddy coins,* a town that is situate in a *nameless* valley, as far as Galaad, *where Gays are simply called Glads.* There was not a village or city that escaped our *destructive* hands: the Lord our God delivered all unto us *without the use of any brown or white road delivery vehicles or defective donkey carts.*

13

Except the land of the children of Ammon, to which we approached not *without ever saying 'Amen' to Ammon':* and all that border *existing* upon *(along)* the Torrent Jeboc, *I say torrent because I have no other word for 'river';* and the cities in the mountains, *and the mountains in the cities,* and all the *metropolitan and rural* places which the Lord our God forbade us *to viciously visit, vex, vacate or vacation.*

Chapter Three

"The Defeat of Og"

The victory over Og, *the weird wizard*/king of Basan *Basin, over* Ruben, *the specialty sandwich king, over* Gad, *Egad,* and half the *"slow-as-molasses"* tribe of Manasses, *the very first battle of our Civil-like War,* receive their possession on the other side of Jordan, the place *and not the future sensational basketball player.* *"But I warn you mentally challenged Israelites; don't ever get the Defeat of Og confused with the feet of Og."*

Then we turned, *took a long-cut,* and went by the way of Basan *Basin:* and Og the King of Basan *Basin, also known as Basin Basan,* came out to meet us with his *dysfunctional* people to fight in Edrai, *where spectator tickets for the battle had already been sold at the lackluster amphitheater arena there.* And the Lord said to me *(Moses):* "Fear him not: because he *(Og)* is delivered into thy hand, with all his people and his *useless* land *too: (for Moses, you have a tremendously huge hand in which all those doltish fools could be delivered):* and thou shalt do to him *(Og and his plethora of numbskull chums)* as thou hast done to Sehon, King of the *sinful amorous* Amorrhites, that dwelt in Hesebon *Cinnebon before we kicked his (their) butt."*

So the Lord our God delivered into our hands, Og also, the King of Basan *Basin,* and all his *dumb-fuck asinine* people: and we utterly destroyed them, *because to be perfectly honest, demolition is what we enjoy most in life doing and then redundantly re-doing.* Wasting all his cities *and their dumpy slums* at one time, there was not a town that *successfully* escaped us, *for we Israelites are the supreme demolition experts of all antiquity:* sixty cities, all the country of Argob/*Shish-ka-bob,* the Kingdom of Og in Basan *Basin, and all those other stupid mother-fuckers in the vicinity too; we adroitly killed all the bastards and bitches in an efficient and expeditious manner!*

All the *defenseless* cities were fenced with very high walls, and with gates and bars, besides innumerable towns that had no walls, *but their shoddy stone houses had no fuckin' dry-wall either.* And we utterly destroyed *and plundered* them, as we had done to Sehon the

15

King of Hesebon *Cinnebon*, destroying every city, men and women and children, *and then we really baked Cinnebon's buns on high heat in an afternoon bonfire. The defenseless destroyed cities now had no walls, and the dead male fighters had no balls, both literally and figuratively.*

But the cattle and the spoils of the cities we took for our prey, *and when we broiled their delicious meat, we felt home on the range. So no one in our invasion could beef to me, greedily arguing, "Where's the fuckin' beef?" And for the sake of confiscation,* we took at that time the land out of the hand of the two kings of the *amorous* Amorrhites, *for both avaricious kings had but one hand, which they sometimes had shared between them.* Their *fucked-up* lands were beyond the Jordan: from the Torrent Arnon unto the Mount Hermon, *where the reclusive Hermon Hermits had once reclusively lived. It is the infertile land* which the Sidonians call Sarion, and the Amorrhites *had called* Sanir: *But we Israelites call all of those blundering weak assholes that don't know shit about shit, "fucked-up!"*

All the cities that are *plainly* situate in the plain, and all the land of Galaad *the Sur* and Basan *Basin* as far as Selcha and Edrai, *all evil* cities of the kingdom of Og in Basan *Basin. Now, I'm (Moses) the foremost authority on Biblical evil, so you must take my word for all that is characterized as truth in this totally masterful Wholly Book of Doo-Doo-Rot-on-Me!*

For only Og, king of Basan *Basin,* remained of the race of the giants, *for the Lord had turned all of the other survivors of that terrible atrocious place into mini-dwarfs and midgets.* Og's bed of iron is shewn, which is in Rabbath of the children of Ammon *Amen,* the *immense object* being nine cubits long, and *four cubits* broad, after the measure of the cubit of a *normal* man's hand, *and so naturally, all had been bedlam with having our violent siege on Og's enormous bed.*

And we possessed the land at that time from Aroer, which is upon the bank of the Torrent Arnon, unto the half of Mount Galaad *of Sur:* and I gave the cities thereof to Rueben and Gad *and also to Egad, because we were not in India, so I refused to be a non-Hebrew Indian giver.*

And I delivered the other part of Galaad *of Sur,* and all Basan *Basin,* the Kingdom of *ugly* Og, to the half tribe of Manasses, all the country of Argob, *along with its zany Ar-goblin ghoulish inhabitants:* and all Basan *Basin* is *now* called the *Lackluster* Land of *former* giants, *mini-dwarfs and midgets.*

Jair, the *berserk* son of Manasses, *who liked to look at female asses too,* possessed all the country of Argob unto the borders of Gessuri, and Machati. *All of the men in Manasses had male asses, and male-type testicles too.* And he *(Jair)* called Basan *Basin* by his own name, Havoth Jair, that is to say, the towns, *villages and indigenous hamlets* of Jair, until this present day, *which is still believed to be political Jairymandering on close election days.*

To Machir also I *gallantly* gave Galaad *of Sur.* And to the tribes of Reuben and Gad *and Egad* I gave of the land of Galaad *of Sur* as far as the Torrent Arnon, half the torrent, and the confines even unto the torrent Jeboc, which is the border of the children of Ammon *Amen, who had a few illegal alien boarders living on the borders. Now unfortunately, all those lazy migrant assholes are vagrant legal refugees and fucked-up illegal aliens too.*

And the plain of the wilderness, and the *adjacent* Jordan *basketball court areas,* and the borders *and boarders* of Cenereth unto the sea of the desert, which is the most salt sea *in the land because it's the only salt sea,* to the foot of Mount Phasga eastward, *for the disadvantaged mountain had had its other foot amputated right before we (the covetous marauding indolent Israelites) had arrived on the bloody battle scene there.*

And I commanded you *erratic ninnies (Israelites)* at that time, *un-eloquently* saying *to you vagrant shit-heads:* "The Lord your God giveth you this land for an inheritance *that none of us belligerent assholes have either earned or deserved, so* go ye well-appointed before your brethren, the *ludicrous* children of Israel, all the strong men of you *that I can count on my thumbs. But I wholeheartedly suggest that the wimpy weak of you ought to commit suicide and end it all right now."*

Leaving your wives and children and cattle, *you Israelites must become insane lemmings and follow my suspect leadership, just like hapless helpless sheep being cunningly led to slaughter.* For I know you have much cattle, and they must remain in the cities *for the distinct purpose of rancid garbage smelling-up the already disgusting ghettos and barrios,* which I *(Moses), through Almighty God's benevolent advice,* have generously *and miraculously* delivered unto you.

Until the *avaricious* Lord gives rest *to the rest* of your *restless* brethren, as He hath *mercifully* given to you: and they *(the one's possessed)* also possess the land, which He *(masculine by preference)* will give them beyond the Jordan *and further beyond the adjacent rinky-dink basketball courts:* then shall every man return to his possession, which I have *fraudulently* given you *as the gifts (spoils) of war.*

I commanded *my commander* Josue also at that time, *specifically* saying *to the ferocious demented warrior:* "Thy eyes have seen what the Lord your God hath done to these two *fucked-up* kings: so will He *(chauvinistic reference)* do to all the kingdoms to which thou shalt pass *with our rabble rebel army of disillusioned looters.* Our new *appropriate* motto is: *Destroy and plunder if you do not give us everything we demand; yes Josue; that is our basic imperative message!"*

Fear them not: for the Lord your God will fight for you, *even though He is invisible and generally claims to be a peaceful pacifist.* And I besought the *always-itinerant* Lord at that time, saying "Lord God, Thou hast begun to show unto Thy *withered senile* servant Thy *total* greatness, and *Thy* most mighty *right* hand, *for You seldom use Your left one for any constructive or destructive purpose;* for there is no other God *(god)* either in Heaven or *(in the)* earth, that is able to do Thy works, or to be compared to Thy strength, *all except maybe that fearsome Hephaestus (Vulcan) fellow residing over there in pagan Greece.*

I will pass over therefore, *even though the Passover is something else, other than what I'm presently speaking about.* Already we will see this excellent land beyond the Jordan Torrent, and this goodly mountain, *I forget its insignificant name,* and Libanus *that will soon wonderfully be all ours for the taking, also. What a tremendous steal that sucker is!*

And the Lord was angry with me on your account, *you asinine Dolts,* and *He* heard me not, but loudly said to me *in either a dream or in an eerie erratic nightmare:* "*Moses,* it is enough: speak no more to Me of this matter *simply because enough is enough!* Go up to the top of Phasga, *and take a peek from the mountain peak.* And cast thy *beady* eyes round-about to the west, and to the north, and to the south, and to the east, *for I think you need some basic direction in a bad way.* And behold it, for thou shalt not *dare* pass *this fantastic barren camel-dung place called* Jordan. *Don't you fathom My' modus operandi Moses? I want the vast wasteland for us to pilfer and then keep!*"

"*But Lord,*" I answered Him in *awful awe,* "*we don't have any deed or title to Jordan, to its courts, or to its incomparable basketball courts either? What the hell should I tell my staunch commander Joshue, even though You' haven't invented the infernal hell inferno yet? I imagine that future place of punishment to be a fiery human furnace for any ignorant Israelite to fear!*"

"Command Josue, and encourage and strengthen him *to perform our will, which is really My' will imposed on you, Moses:* for he *(Josue)* shall *awkwardly* go before this people, and shall divide unto them the land which thou shalt see *from your brief peek from atop the mountain peak.*"

And *then* we *nervously pitched and hurled our tents and* abode *somewhere* in the *sultry* valley over against the Temple of Phogor, *which, if my faulty memory serves me correctly, was not-too-far distant from what later became known as 'Shirlee Temple'.*

Chapter Four

"Advantages of Fidelity"

Moses exhorteth the people to keep God's Commandments *in a safe place out of the reach of impressionable children and non-impressionable pedophiles:* particularly to fly idolatry *out the window, even though we dim-witted tribes (the Israelites) were a rabble pack of wandering wondering nomads having no huts or houses with either windows or doors to fly idolatry out of.*

Indeed, I shudder at the thought of worrying about all those prospective open shutters. The Lord *has* appointeth three cities of refuge *for us fugitives-from-Egyptian-justice to spoil, yes, we on-the-move refugees must settle* on that *sun-less* side of the Jordan. *It is truly only a degree harder to appointeth cities than to appointeth qualified Hebrew leaders among those neurotic psychotic asylum maniacs who are accompanying me on this rather futile, extremely exhausting journey.*

And now, O Israel, *even though an imaginary wandering country has no ears, or even any disfigured ear lobes, yes my* country, hear the Commandments and judgments which I teach thee' *straight from my delirious undependable subconscious:* that doing them, thou mayst live, and entering in, mayst possess the land which the Lord, the God of your *three* fathers, will give you *until either Heaven or Hell is allowed for us nondescript nomads to dwell in.*

You shall not add to the word that I speak to you, *including the thousands of words I've mysteriously added into this narrative from my countless inexplicable mental delusions;* neither shall you take away from it, *you desperate horde (hoarding herd) of guilty, compulsive thieves and amateur on-the-lam plunderers:* keep the Commandments of the Lord your God which I command you, *before I am predictably committed by Josue to solitary confinement.*

Your *blurry spiteful* eyes have seen all that the Lord hath done against Beelphegor, how He hath destroyed all his worshipers from among you, *so watch out all you other flagrant violators out there, for you shall soon be destroyed in a similar fashion if you don't wise-up and heed my persistent threats.* But you that adhere to the Lord your God *and implicitly trust in my erudite lectures and in my suspect integrity,* you *freaks-of-nature* are all alive until this present day *and will not arbitrarily perish as did the other apathetic moronic transgressors who were fucking-around causing major trouble among you.*

Abandon your false god statues, for you *facetious fools* know that I have taught you *moral* statutes, and in terms of justices, *without any human Chief Justices overriding me and consequently determining (through Amendments and not Commandments) what constitutes immoral civil laws,* as the Lord my God hath commanded me to *instruct you, the clumsy mindless masses:* so shall *you shallow fools* do them *(the Ten Commandments)* in the land which you shall *involuntarily* possess.

And you shall observe, and fulfill them in practice, *for practice makes perfect.* For this is your wisdom, *and if you wish to be a 'wiz', then cease being 'dumb' and therefore Assholes, listen to my profundity.* And *to achieve* understanding in the sight of nations, that hearing all these *seemingly illogical* precepts *I am currently preaching,* they *(pagan doubters)* may *plausibly* say: "Behold a wise and understanding people, a great nation *of absolute repulsive retards.*"

Neither is there any other nation so great, that hath gods so nigh them, as our God is present to all our petitions *and to all our unwritten writs, for we Israelites hardly know how to fuckin' speak, let alone know how to friggin' write.* For what other nation is there so renowned that hath *in their methods such totally meaningless* ceremonies, incomprehensible rituals *and also such foul-tasting victuals,* along with *a complement of* just *and unjust* judgments, and all the *convoluted* law *that we must reluctantly follow and obey,* which I will set forth this day before our eyes, *despite the fact that I cannot write and despite the fact that paper and pencils haven't been created yet! So therefore O Israel, you must believe my oral bullshit or else be doomed to death and final destruction!*

Keep thyself therefore, and thy soul carefully *inside your frail feeble bodies.* Forget not the words that thy eyes have seen, *erratic words flying out of my mouth and wildly flitting-around all over the fuckin' place.* And let them not go out of thy heart *(even though those questionable, illogical words are already present in your eyes and in your souls)* all the days of thy *remaining* life. *Forget the unimportant daughters and the insignificant grand-daughters!* Thou shalt teach the Lord's laws to thy sons and to thy grandsons, *who no doubt will be even more stupid than you mental and emotional egocentric freaks currently are.*

From the day in which thou didst stand *for seventy-six hours* before the Lord thy God in Horeb, when the Lord *selectively* spoke to me *and not to you pathetic reckless masses,* saying: *"O Moses,* call together the people unto Me, that they may hear My *wonderful irrational* words, and may learn to fear Me all the time that they live on the Earth, and may teach their children *all kinds of irrelevant information also. For Moses, this method of fear and inculcation that I employ is precisely how 'we' shall control the mindless masses in the near and in the distant future.*

And you came to the foot of the mount, *standing immediately next to the big toe's lengthy dirt-laden toe-nail,* which burned even unto Heaven: and there was darkness, and a cloud and obscurity in it, *for as you are quite aware Moses, I despise and abhor dirty big toe toe-nails. The reprehensible things must always be shrouded in obscurity.*

And the Lord spoke to you *(Israelites)* from the midst of the *raging bush* fire. You heard the *omnipotent* voice of His words, but you saw not any form *in the bush fire* at all, *but I (Moses) heard the Lord's entire lecture even though I had soft mashed potatoes stuffed inside my ears.* And the Lord showed you His covenant, *during a 'Really Big Shew' that you Israelite dolts never appreciated,* which He commanded you to do, and the ten words *(this allusion might be a gross mathematical miscalculation)* that He wrote upon two tables of stone, *for the Omnipotent Lord knows how to write but will not teach either me or you how to communicate in that sophisticated advanced academic fashion.*

And He commanded me at that time that I should teach you the *standard* ceremonies and judgments which you shall do in the land, that you shall possess, *but do not understand one iota.* Keep therefore your souls carefully *somewhere stored inside your grotesque deformed bodies.* You saw not any similitude in the day that the Lord God spoke to you in Horeb from the midst of the *spectacular* fire, *but I assure you, regardless of my severe dual retina degeneration, I had keenly observed (while you hare-brains didn't) that both the Lord and His Words were on fire!*

Lest perhaps being deceived you might make you a graven similitude, or evil image of male or female, *preferably sinful nude female images.* The similitude of any beasts that are upon the Earth, or of birds, that fly under Heaven, *or any other absurd bullshit like that is strictly prohibited and could result in sudden divine extermination.*

Or of creeping things *that give us the creeps,* that *slimily* move on the Earth, or of fishes, *whales and lobsters* that abide in the waters *in   massive yet-to-be-seen subterranean oceans* underneath the Earth: Lest perhaps lifting-up thy eyes to Heaven, thou see the sun and the moon, and all the stars of Heaven *and of Fantasy Hollywood,* and being deceived by error, thou adore and serve them, *especially the future liberal Fantasy Hollywood stars,* which the Lord thy God *will have allowed being created* for the service of all the nations, that are under Heaven, *performed   just to distract us from the real truth and also enacted to mischievously piss us all off while simultaneously, sportively playing some sort of supernatural prank on us rather limited inept humans.*

But the *determined* Lord hath taken you and brought you out of the iron furnaces of Egypt, *and while the blasted heat was on, so to speak,* to make you His people of inheritance, *His luckless beneficiaries of nothing but useless desert land that belongs to other useless tribes of hostile pagan people already settled here,* as it is this present day. *And some wondrous day the educated Egyptians might even learn how to produce steel in their blasted bronze and iron blast furnaces.*

And the Almighty Lord was *especially* angry with me *(Moses)* for your *challenging and somewhat sophisticated anti-religious* words, and He swore *(without a Bible)* that I should not pass over the Jordan *and its adjacent basketball courts,* nor enter into the excellent *barren desert* land, which He will give you at His discretion.

Behold I shall die in this land, *which I can't wait to fuckin' do, and because of the Lord's indomitable will,* I shall not pass over the Jordan: But you shall pass the River, and possess the goodly *goodie-goodie* land, *possibly led there in triumph by the inimitable Archangel Michael of Jordan.* Beware lest thou ever forget the Divine Covenant of the Lord thy God, which He hath made with thee, *but actually, only with me while I was merrily smoking and inhaling marijuana:* and make not to thyself a graven likeness of those things which the Lord hath forbidden to be made, *like marvelous images of nude lesbians, for example:* Because the Lord thy God is a consuming fire, a jealous God *Who kicks ass and Who kills evil sinners and sinful enemies alike when He feels compelled to do so.*

If you shall beget sons and grandsons, *beget them while the getting's good,* and abide *and reside* in the *stolen* land, and being deceived, make to yourselves any similitude, committing evil before the Lord your God, to provoke him to wrath, *for it would be much better and less painful for you idiots to simply commit mass suicide.*

I call this day Heaven and Earth to witness, *(for lack of a better more accurate expression),* that you shall quickly perish out of the land, which, when you have passed over the Jordan, which you shall possess *after drinking the fabled river's black magic water.* You shall not dwell therein long, but the Lord will *certainly* destroy you *before you ever die of thirst.* And *through His notorious unmerciful vengeance,* scatter you *hard-headed lunatics* among all nations, and you shall remain a few among the nations *for more than a few years,* to which the Lord shall lead you *and discriminately punish you, so if you indiscreetly violate the omniscient 10 Commandments and then egregiously sin, you should also learn how to become receptive masochists ready for torture.*

And there *across the Jordan* you shall serve *false and phony* gods *and evil sex goddesses,* that were framed with men's hands: wood and stone *images having long erect penises and displaying big flabby tits too, upon each and every fucked-up statue,* that neither see, nor hear, nor eat, nor smell *a damned thing.*

And when thou shalt seek there the Lord thy God, thou shalt find Him *among the false nude sex images, even though He will have no physical or sex image Himself:* yet so, if thou seek Him *as an existing Wandering Spirit* with all thy heart, and all the affliction of thy *troubled mortal-sinned* soul, *He will amazingly descend from the upper atmosphere and comfort your suffering spirits.* After all the things aforesaid shall find thee, in the latter time, thou shalt return to the Lord thy God, and shalt hear His *Omnipresent* Voice for the first time, *for quite frankly, I'm excessively tired of hearing It alone all these long difficult years.*

Because the Lord thy God is *occasionally* a merciful God, He will not leave thee *stranded in caravan traffic,* nor altogether destroy thee, nor forget the covenant, by which He swore to thy fathers, *who are all fuckin' dead and now existing nowhere, for it is common knowledge that dead people don't know anything at all, no matter where the fuck they're buried.* Ask of the days of old *when oldies music and oldies' psalms were popular,* that have been before thy time from the day that God created man upon the Earth, from one end of Heaven to the other end thereof, *all over the fuckin' accursed planet,* if ever there was done the like thing, or it hath been known at any *peculiar past* time. *Thank the Lord for marvelous Cloud Technology!*

That a *doubting egotistical* people should hear the Voice of God speaking out of the midst of fire, as thou hast heard and lived, *is definitely far beyond the normal realms of academic and scientific knowledge.* If God ever did so as to go, and take to Himself a nation out of the midst of nations by temptations, by signs, and by wonders, by fight, and by a strong hand, *or by means of any other dumb shit activity,* and by stretched-out arm, and by horrible visions according to all the *fantastic* things that the Lord your God did for you in Egypt, before thy eyes, *then this obviously incomprehensible further action will make about as much sense as the Wholly Book of Genesis and the Wholly Book of Exodus ever did.*

That thou mightest know that the Lord He is God, and there is no other besides *(or beside)* Him. From Heaven He made thee to hear His *booming* voice *that up to now only I Moses have heard and discerned,* that He might teach thee *as He has effectively instructed me in the puzzling ways of religion.* And upon Earth, He showed thee His exceeding great fire, and thou didst hear His words out of the midst of the fire, *all of you maniacs aspiring and wishing to become destructive pyromaniacs while sinfully pursuing the conquest of old and new flames, whose pussies you screw and chew are also indeed excessively sinful.*

Because He loved thy' fathers, and chose their seed after them, *their erect penises being more fertile than their limp minds.* And He *benevolently* brought thee out of Egypt *with all your testicle sperms and all your ovary eggs fully intact,* going before thee with His great power, *enabling you degenerate mutant mutates to screw and to multiple and add to His burgeoning population, but not counter-productively to divide and subtract, let alone divide and conquer.*

To destroy at thy coming, very great nations, and stronger than thou art *with them having more advanced technology, weapons along with avante-garde science, math', language arts and social studies too,* and to bring thee *primitive post-cavemen into His privileged divine company,* and *ultimately* give thee their *valueless* (the vanquished conquered people) land for a *charitable tax-deductible* possession, as thou seest *fit to use* at this present day.

Know therefore this *special* day *on the Hebrew Prehistoric Calendar,* and think in thy heart that the Lord He is God in Heaven above, and in the Earth beneath, and there is no other god *anywhere else in the infinite Universe, except only our parochial Earth Creator and Lord.* Keep His *arbitrary* precepts and *His capricious* Commandments, which I *now* command *(and demand)* thee: that it may be well with thee, and *with* thy children after thee, and thou mayst remain a long time upon the *invaded* land, which the Lord thy God will give thee *after you have successfully encroached, invaded and vanquished the sandy worthless territory.*

Then Moses set aside three cities beyond the Jordan at the *lower* east side, that anyone *without fleas* might flee to them who should *intentionally or unintentionally* kill his neighbor, *either willingly or* unwillingly, and *the victim* was not his enemy a day or two before, and that he *(the murderer)* might escape to one of these cities *for committing bloody murder, also known as "scarlet homicide."*

Bosor, *located* in the *vast* wilderness, which is situate in the plains of the tribe of Reuben *the Distinguished Sandwich King:* and Ramoth in Galaad near *Galahad,* which is in the tribes of *those villains* Gad *and Egad:* and Golan in Basan *Basin,* which is in the tribe of Manasses, *located way up in the heights, but not in the lofty heights of hypocrisy.*

This is the *prescribed* law that Moses *(me)* set before the children of Israel. *How my physical country could give birth to children without a physical, only the all-powerful Lord knows the answer to this incredible secret mystery!*

And these are the testimonies and ceremonies and judgments, which He spoke to the children of Israel, when they came out of Egypt *without any skilled chiropractors in their numbers, but for some uncanny evasive obscure explanation, only I (author/bard Moses) had heard the ominous articulations being uttered.*

Beyond the Jordan in the valley over against the Temple of Phogor, in the land of Sehon, King of the Amorrhites, that dwelt in Hesebon *Cinnebon,* whom Moses *(I, me)* slew *with a dull putty knife.* And the children of Israel coming out of Egypt, *fortunately not being a-nile-a-lated as already mentioned,* possessed his (Sehon's) land, and the land of Og, *the crazy wizard/*King of Basan *Basin, often called Basin Basan, and also possessed* the land of the two kings of the Amorrhites, *who as all the gossiping locals know, were dedicated gay faggots living and practicing sodomy* beyond the Jordan, somewhere towards the *redundant* eastern rising of the sun.

From Aroer, which is situate upon the bank of the Torrent Arnon, unto Mount Sion, which is also called Hermon, *the condemned plateau where a plethora of sinful gay hermits mount each other morning, noon and night after giving each other full moons.*

All the plain beyond the Jordan at the *lower* east side, unto the sea of the wilderness, and unto the foot of Mount Phasga is barren, *but the lustful bastards and bitches that live there and who hump and pump there are certainly not barren whatsoever!*

Chapter Five

"The 10 Commandments Restated"

The immortal Ten Commandments are repeated *and explained by me, Moses.*

And Moses *(me)* called all Israel, and said to them *en masse because he (I, me) liked speaking to whole nations when I (me) wasn't only listening to the Omniscient Lord's astounding rhetoric:* Hear, O Israel, the ceremonies and judgments, which I speak *with only one mouth* into your *millions of* ears this day: learn them, and complete them in work *or else face the dire consequences that shall be administered upon you miserable narrow-minded shit-heads, the retribution genuinely described as Divine Retribution.*

The Lord our God made a covenant with us in Horeb, but only I *(Moses) remember the unilateral contract's complicated clauses, both main and subordinate clauses.* He made not the covenant with our fathers, but with us, who are now present and living, *although He liked our deceased three fathers (Abraham, Isaac and Jacob) much more than He presently likes any of us! As you mediocre dimwits don't recall,* He spoke to us face-to-face (but not cheek-to-cheek) in the mount *(not on it), bellowing moral wisdom* out of the midst of *infernal* fire. *If you remember that historic day, we were all wearing filthy robes and not our scruffy blazers.*

I *(Moses)* was the mediator and stood between the Lord and you at that time, to interpret for you His *glorious* words, for you feared the fire, and went not up into the mountain *forest flames, afraid that the dangerous flares from the burning bush would enter and cauterize your all-too-vulnerable assholes,* and He *at the time dramatically* said *the following:*

I, the Lord, am your God, Who' brought you out of the *condemned* land of Egypt, that *horrible* place of *abject* slavery, *and you were professionally led to a hostile hot sultry eastern desert where you and your minions almost starved to death. I mercifully took you and your all-too-numerous dregs out of slavery in Egypt so that the Israelites could be My' special exclusive possessions. Get it Moses?"*

"Is there really a distinction as to the various types of slavery?"
Moses (I) sincerely requested knowing. "Is Yours' any better than the
Pharaoh's?"

The Lord looked upon (me) Moses "with deaf ears and also with
blind eyes." Then He' said, "You shall not have other gods besides
Me' *Moses, for I am THE LORD of the universe that dwells as a*
lonely Hermit on this remote desert mountain hundreds of miles
away from any remnants of organized civilization. You shall not *idly*
carve *dolls, puppets or* idols for yourselves in the shape of anything
in the sky or on the Earth, either below or under the waters beneath
the Earth," *the Lord distinctly commanded. "If you do those naughty*
bad things, I will quickly become very envious and resentful and then
visit you and the hapless Israelites with such mass destruction you
cannot imagine. But unfortunately, this stubborn recalcitrance, it's in
your DNA."

"DNA?" I (Moses) asked.

"Yes, in your Dumb Ass Naughtiness!"

"So what else is new?" Moses (I) countered. "It all sounds like
the same old past rot, simply re-packaged and repeated in the
present and also in the future tense tenses! In all due respect Lord,
try to be a little more original and a little less aboriginal next time."

"You shall not bow down before them *(the false god-idols with*
long penises and flabby tits) or worship them," the Lord *bluntly* said.
"For I am the Lord your God, and I am a jealous God, inflicting
punishment for their *(the inconsistent recalcitrant Israelites')*
fathers' wickedness on the children of those *vile dissenters* who hate
Me, *right* down to the third and fourth generation."

"Now why or how could anyone down here on Earth possibly
hate You?" Moses (me) responded with a degree of indignation and
sarcasm. "Especially all the living Egyptians and the accursed
Israelites and the innocent Canaanites, who all wish that You would
permanently move to another world somewhere far from this
repugnant Earth that You claim to have created!"

The unruffled and undeterred Lord was so engrossed in His own
sensational oratory that He was unaware of Moses (me) saying

anything at all. "But bestowing mercy down to the thousandth generation, *if men still have sperm and women still manufacture eggs in that distant era,*" the Lord *emphatically* stated, "on the children who love Me and keep *My Demandments, er, I'm sorry there Moses,* My Ten Commandments, *I shall bless and favor.*"

"Exactly, what are these new Demandments, er, Commandments?" Moses (I) laconically asked. "I hope they aren't too severe or Draconian! I mean, it's bad enough that the Israelites now lead a Spartan existence without much in the way of material comforts!"

"Number One, you shall not take the Name of the Lord your God in vain *no matter how frustrated you become at My casually playing power games with your meaningless lives,"* the all-powerful Voice *emphatically stated.* "For the Lord will not leave unpunished him who takes His *(My)* name in vain."

"I know a half million Israelites' who are doomed to immediate extinction because of Your' current provocative threat!" Moses (I) frightfully answered the Lord. "You have been cursed and cussed by Your' chosen people many more times than You have cunningly cursed the Israelites and the Egyptians with plagues, suffering and illusionary 'hardship' mirages in the hot sultry eastern desert."

"Moses, remember to keep holy the Sabbath day," the Lord reminded *his thoroughly confused listener.* "Six days you may labor and do all your work, but the seventh day is sacred and belongs to the Lord your God."

"That's when Jethro Reuel, Homer Samson and I can cash in big on the seventh day, the fabulous donations and contributions we've been receiving from our various wild threats," Moses (I) confessed to the Almighty Lord. "We can become filthy rich without working, a foolproof fantastic pyramid-scheme that even the new anonymous Pharaoh over there in Egypt would obviously envy!"

"No work may be done then, either by you *down by the bayou with Homer (a future Greek) and Jethro (priest of Midian).* Your son or daughter may not work, or your male or female slave *or sex slave of either sex may not work either,"* the Lord sternly lectured. "No work shall be done by the beast or by the *legal or illegal* alien who lives with you, *even if you regard your ugly slutty wife as a beastly legal or illegal alien.*"

"*I don't think these new rules are going to set too well with the average Israelite's mercurial psyche,*" Moses (I) *sincerely replied, shaking his (my) head side to side to illustrate his (my) obvious displeasure and doubt. "The people don't even like Jethro Reuel's rules let alone these new mandatory ones established by You' nowhere near a bayou or a stupid tax levy!"*

"*They aren't rules!*" *the Lord bellowed. "They are laws! My' personal Commandments!*" *He thundered with menacing authority.* "In six *magnificent* days the Lord (Me) made Heaven and Earth, the sea and all that is in them."

"*Why do You keep talking about Yourself and Your various achievements in the third person Voice when You should be speaking to me in the first person?*" *Moses (I) brazenly criticized. "How are the Israelites going to ever master fundamental grammar and communications' skills when You keep abusing the language almost as effectively as You have abused the Hebrews since the time of our besieged Patriarch Abraham?*"

"But on the last day, He' *(I)* rested," *the Lord proceeded as He described an event from the distant past.* "That is why the Lord has blessed the Sabbath Day and has decided to make it holy! *Now at least I have named one day of the week for all to be able to know and revere its basic identity.*"

"*That proves that You too have limitations if You had to rest after creating the Earth and the sea after six days of strenuous labor,*" Moses (I) *perceptively and boldly recognized and challenged. "You too are not quite as immortal and invincible as You Lord have portended and pretended to be! It seems that You too have Your glaring limitations!*"

The Lord proceeded with sharing His eloquent repertoire in spite of Moses' (my) justified objections. "Next, honor your father and your mother that you may have a long life in the land that the Lord, your God is giving you," *the Voice communicated from the smoky burning bush. "Honor them no matter how much they may have used and abused and dishonored you in the past!*"

"Yeah!" agreed Moses (me), "just like the Israelites have to pay homage and servitude to You for mercilessly busting our stones and deflating our women's tits for all these hundreds of years since Abraham 'erred' and took his family out of Ur. How much more travail can we possibly endure?"

"Next, you shall not kill *or imitate the way that I took care of the Egyptians, the entire population of the Earth during the time of Noah, during the spectacular destruction of Sodom and Gomorrah, and of course, during the brutal massacre of the previously invincible Egyptian army crossing the Red Sea."*

"And next on My agenda Moses, you shall not commit adultery, *and I am still investigating into other perverted sexual behavior such as but not limited to pre-marital sex, the licentious deportments of the gay and lesbian community, and also, sexually active teenagers having wanton sex with married adults and with eunuchs of all age brackets."*

"Next, thou shall not steal, *especially after you confiscate the land of Canaan from the Canaanites as I have continually promised Abraham, Isaac, Jacob to own and possess, and as I now promise you and the illiterate and loathsome indolent Israelites."*

"Next on my short list, you *Moses* shall not bear false witness *against your neighbor, especially when I might happen to be your neighbor. The only exceptions are when your neighbors happen to be the conniving Canaanites, the inane insane family of Amalek or the berserk faggot relatives of gay Egyptian transgender aristocrats. Then in those special cases, bear all the false witness you want, even if there are no witnesses."*

"In addition Moses, a new law is that You shall not covet your neighbor's *(Israelite's)* house, *but if your neighbor is a Canaanite, a follower of Amalek or an Egyptian having her bloody period, become instantly prejudiced and burn the damned residence to the ground with the occupant still inside if you so desire."*

"Also Moses, you shall not covet your neighbor's *(Israelite's)* wife, *but if your neighbor is a Canaanite, that cad Amalek, or a crazy gay Egyptian bothering you, do anything you want to your neighbor and to his good-looking wife."*

And furthermore, do not covet his male or female slave, nor his ox or his ass *or his male or female slave's ass either.* Do not covet anything else *(goods)* that belongs to him *(even an Israelite), but if your neighbor is a Canaanite, is Amalek, or is a dastardly gay or lesbian Egyptian, then kindly ignore the sacred principles associated with this last Demandment, er, I mean Commandment."*

When the people *(the ingrate, self-centered Hebrews)* had witnessed the *Lord's grand finale* thunder *and accompanying pyrotechnic* lightning *demonstrations,* the *archangel's shrill* trumpet blast and the mountain *subsequently* smoking *a gigantic marijuana joint,* they all feared and trembled *simultaneously, just like they all always habitually spoke and chanted at the same damned time.*

So they *(the easily astounded Israelites)* took up a position much farther away and said to Moses *(me) all together from a mile distant,* "You speak to us, and we will listen. *We don't want to be blasted with lightning and instantaneously electrocuted up our asses into another unknown dimension by our unpredictable and erratic-behaving Supreme Lord. Or else we shall die, which on second thought, might actually be a miraculous blessing in disguise and also in addition, the correct solution to the immediate problems associated with living in this abominable wasteland!" all half million or so desert-dwellers and direction-less Israelite meanderers recited together to Moses (me) in a discordant chorus from a full mile away.*

Moses (I) *audaciously* answered the *frightened moronic assembled* people *by uttering,* "Do not be afraid, *you petrified stupid assholes!* God has come to you only to test you *(your mettle)* and put His *dreaded* fear upon you, lest you should sin *and enjoy yourselves for the first time in your hideous condemned boring lives. I've concluded in my final analysis that God wants to determine if you donkeys all have 'heavy mettle'!"*

Still the *apprehensive* people remained at a distance, *not knowing who was crazier, Moses (me) or their Lord thundering away inside a dark rain cloud that had been swirling around on the horizon.* Moses *(me)* then approached the cloud where God was *presumably whirling and rotating, and the New Age patriarch (me) was virtually in a trance.*

The *turbulent* Lord told Moses (me), "Thus shall you speak *to My chosen people*, the *lame-minded* Israelites: 'You have seen for yourselves that I have spoken to you from Heaven', *which presently is all Mine and not a place that I wish to share with you lowly dull Israelites, either dead or alive right now. Truthfully,' the Lord said, 'Heaven is too good for inferior caliber idiots of low ilk such as yours!* But I warn you *stubborn fools;* do not make anything to rank with Me; neither gods of silver nor gods of gold shall you make for yourselves'."

"It sounds like You're a little too paranoid about experiencing religious competition and diversity," Moses (I) bravely challenged. *"A tad lightly neurotic and jealous too, if I may add!"*

"An altar of earth you shall make for Me *that shall never be altered.* Upon it you shall sacrifice your holocausts, *for as you know Moses, the Lord likes and values holocausts, but only here on altars in the Old Testament. That particular attitude, however, may drastically change in the future.* Sacrifice your peace offerings too, your *favorite* sheep and your *prized* oxen, *and your 'oxen-morons too'! Sacrifice everything that you deem worthwhile to Me!"* the Lord haughtily declared. "In whatever place *or temple* that I choose for the remembrance of My' name, I will come to you and bless you. *But whatever you do, don't sin in the synagogue!"*

"Your blessings are really much like wicked curses," Moses (I) *injected into the rather interesting verbal exchange, "and if the Israelites and I could have our druthers, we would prefer to be cursed rather than be blessed 'by You' on any blue bayou or tax levy provided by You. Then some good might result from the nasty curse You would be administering."*

"If you make an altar of stone for Me," *the Lord deliberately interrupted while ignoring the almost delirious New Age Patriarch's (me) comment,* "do not build it of cut stone, for by putting *(a human)* tool to it you *therefore* desecrate it. *I really don't desire to see man develop tools, machines and weapons that might eventually rival My supremacy over the primitive post-Stone Age pastoral shepherding Israelites that you arrogantly lead and represent. That's why I had a major problem with the adamant gay, lesbian and trans-gender Egyptians. They had civilization, education, science and plenty of advanced technology too in spite of their abundant immorality!"*

35

"Is there anything else to discuss and dictate for me' to consider, Boss?" Moses (I) gingerly inquired while trembling greatly. "If You' don't extinguish me, I'm afraid that the 'don't give a crap' Israelites will take turns kicking my fat wrinkled ass right into the nearest active volcano!"

"Yes, *as a matter of fact there is something else Moses,*" the Lord *loudly* replied. "You shall not go up by steps to My altar, on which you must not be indecently uncovered. *Whatever you do Moses, watch your damned step all the way up there or else your altar life will be severely altered!*"

Chapter Six

"Review of the Law"

This is an exhortation to the love of God, and obedience to His *established* law. These are *reviews of* the precepts, and ceremonies, and judgments, which the Lord your God commanded that I should teach you *crude uncultured Israelites, as if you are at all remotely interested in personal sacrifice and in obeying rules and laws that often limit individual pleasure,* and that you should do them in the land into which you pass over to *passively* possess it.

That thou mayst fear *first and love second* the Lord thy God, and keep all His commandments and precepts, which I command thee, and thy sons, and thy grandsons, all the days of thy life, that thy days may be prolonged *as you unhappily live in a fascist religious theocracy.* Hear, O Israel, and observe to do the *freedom-limiting* things which the Lord hath commanded thee, that it may be well with thee, and thou mayst be greatly multiplied *because you obey these totally suspect principles,* as the Lord the God of thy *three non-triplet* fathers hath promised thee, a land flowing with milk and honey *without any cows or bees ever existing there.*

Hear, O Israel, the Lord our God is one Lord. Thou shalt love the Lord thy God with thy whole heart, *because we Israelites don't believe in half-hearted love.* And *you should* love the Lord with thy whole soul, and with thy whole strength, *but I (Moses) am exempt from these inane flaccid pledges.* And these words which I command thee on this' day, shall be in thy heart, *blocking all of your auricles, oracles and ventricles too. So if you do not love the Lord, you are certain to get high blood pressure and die from cardiac arrest.*

And thou shalt tell them (the 10 Commandments) to thy children, and thou shalt meditate upon them sitting in thy house, and walking on thy journey, sleeping and rising. *Your already-bored children should never hear anything else from your redundant lips except these strict laws of no-no behavior.*

And thou shalt bind them as a sign on thy hand, and they shall be and shall move between thy eyes, *nose, mouth, ears, assholes, testicles, tits and ovaries too.*

37

And thou shalt write them (the laws) in the entry, and on the doors of thy house, *after learnable standardized alphabets are finally invented and after everyone learns how to read chicken-scratch, Sanskrit, hieroglyphics, lower-glyphics and the like.*

And when the Lord thy God shall have brought thee into the land *with me (Moses) as your prophet guide,* for which He *solemnly* swore to thy fathers Abraham, Isaac, and Jacob *(Aren't you extremely lucky to have three fathers instead of one?):* and shall have given thee great and goodly *goodie-goodie good and plenty* cities, which thou didst not build, *or even have to build because the all-too-convenient cities had already been adeptly raided, pilfered and stolen.*

Houses full of riches, which thou didst not set up, cisterns which thou didst not dig, vineyards and olive yards, which thou didst not plant, *all of these easily purloined things were yours for the taking, since that was the Lord's cherished will.* And thou shalt have eaten and be full, *and the next day, thou shall be full of shit too because of your massive gluttony!*

Take heed diligently, *you rambunctious psycho' Alzheimer and Parkinson fanatics,* lest thou forget the Lord, who brought thee out of the land of Egypt, out of the house of bondage, *which was similar to one of those infamous kinky Sado-Masochism Clinics featuring all kinds of excruciating agonizing torture.* Thou shalt fear the Lord thy God, and shalt serve Him only, and thou shalt swear by His name *but not swear His name in public or in private, or in thought or in deed.*

You shall not go after the strange gods of all the nations, that are round about you, *for those deceitful pagan gods are ungodly:* Because the Lord thy God is a jealous God in the midst of thee: lest at any time the wrath of the Lord thy God be kindled against thee, *just like the burning bush on the mountain had been magically and mysteriously kindled,* and take thee away from the face of the Earth, *and who the hell knows where you'll be transported to then? Choose known Earth over unknown oblivion!*

Thou shalt not tempt the Lord thy God, as thou tempted Him in the place of temptation. *But the main problem of my flimsy premise is that there are millions-upon-millions of places of temptation all over the fuckin' known and unknown world. There may even be myriad 'temptations' in oblivion too, just ask 'my girl' friend Mosanna in the Lowest!*

Keep the precepts of the Lord thy God, and the testimonies and ceremonies which He hath commanded thee, *or else be prepared to suffer greatly, maybe by having your testicles evaporate or your tits disintegrate, or perhaps having your exposed rectums rectified when eliminating dispensable malodorous fecal matter.*

And do that which is pleasing and good in the sight of the Lord, that it may be well with thee s*o that you will be allowed to enjoy experiencing (as a reward) a super orgasm once every decade or so:* and going in thou mayst possess the goodly land, concerning which the Lord swore to thy *three non-triplet* fathers, *who are all dead, buried, disintegrated and unrewarded by an afterlife. So much for loyal Heavenly obedience!*

That He, *the vindictive Lord,* would destroy all thy enemies before thee, as He hath spoken *and predicted.* And when thy son shall ask thee tomorrow, saying: "What mean these *dumb-fuck* testimonies, and ceremonies and judgments, which the Lord our God hath *coyly* commanded us *to obey?"* Thou shalt say to him *(or to her, even if she's a trans-gender transvestite asshole):* "We were bondmen of the *anonymous no-name* Pharaoh in Egypt, and the Lord brought us out of Egypt with a strong hand *to play either poker or blackjack."*

And He wrought signs and wonders great and very grievous in Egypt against *the anonymous* Pharaoh, and all his' house, in our sight, *so then no more Vaudeville shows could be staged at the Palace.* And He brought us out from thence, that He might bring us in and give us the *invaded and stolen* land *at His gracious generosity,* concerning which He *solemnly* swore to our *three non-triplet* fathers.

And the Lord commanded that we should do all these *austere asinine* ordinances, and *that we should* fear the Lord our God, that it might be well with us all the days of our life *(lives),* as it is at this *momentous* day *in Hebrew unrecorded history.*

And He will be merciful to us, if we keep and do all His *capricious* precepts before the Lord our God, as He hath commanded us. *But why should we loyally obey these Ten Commandments when we will not be rewarded by any hereafter after demonstrating our steadfast allegiance to the capricious Laws? In retrospect, both life and death are not fair!*

Chapter Seven

"The Destruction of the Pagans"

There is no league nor fellowship to be made with the Canaanites: *those rowdy pin-headed pagan barbarians don't like sports conferences, nor do they get involved with gossipy community civic clubs.* God promiseth His people His blessing and assistance, *but only* if they keep His Commandments *and completely ignore the more sophisticated culture and civilization of the very damned heathen smart-ass Canaanites.*

When the Lord thy God shall have brought thee into the land *(Is this ridiculously monotonous theme getting a little too redundant, or what?),* which thou art going in to possess *against the uncooperative savage smart-ass Canaanites,* and shall have destroyed many nations before thee, *among them* the *hostile heathen* Hethites, and the gruesome Gergezites, *and the perpetually sneezing Gesundheits,* and the *amorous* Amorrhites, and the *cannibalistic* Canaanites, and the *fucked-up* Pherezites, and the Jebusites, *and also the unruly Jeb-Bushites, all together,* nations much more numerous than thou art, and stronger than thou *Israelites in terms of kicking ass, but more specifically, kicking our ass.*

And the Lord thy God shall have delivered them *(the villainous pagans)* to thee, thou shalt utterly destroy them, *but only if the perverted enemies are first delivered by legitimate pediatricians.* Thou shalt make no *major or minor* league with them, nor show *genuine* mercy to them, nor should your *Sisters of Mercy show mercy to them, the annoying clowns and buffoons that these troublesome heathen pagans are.*

Neither shalt thou make marriages *(straight or gay)* with them, *the despicable foreigners, since they are somewhat superior to us in math', science and in other forms of irrelevant academic bullshit.* Thou shalt not give thy daughter to his son, *step-son, or half-son,* nor take his daughter for thy son, *step-son or half-son. But if you have more than one son or one daughter, regrettably, I don't have any advice for you about your other wild card dumb-shit offspring.*

For she *(the pagan bitch)* will turn away thy son, *step-son or half-son* from following me *(Moses),* that he *(the hypothetical pagan bastard)* may rather serve strange gods, and the wrath of the Lord will be kindled, and will quickly destroy thee, thy son, *thy step-son and thy half-son, partly on my behalf.*

But thus rather shall you deal with them *without playing cards, that is to say,* dealing with *your hypothetical disloyal family betrayers:* Destroy their altars, *alter their pagan tabernacles,* break their *expensive false-god* statues, *bust their heathen balls, deflate their diabolical tits* and cut down their *productive* groves, and burn their graven things *to a bacon-like crisp, especially their false god statues with the fully disgusting long erect curved penises.*

Because thou art a holy people to the Lord thy God, *you peabrained Israelites must wholly understand His intentions and my (Moses) motives.* The Lord thy God hath chosen thee *in a celestial lottery,* to be His peculiar people *un-representative* of all *gay and lesbian* peoples *(ostracized assholes and jerk-offs)* that are upon the Earth, *including all the enumerable trans-gender misfits and all of their associated perverted transvestite minions cluttering-up the entire friggin' planet.*

Not because you surpass all nations in number, *you wimpy and feckless minority,* is the Lord joined unto you, and hath chosen you *in the celestial raffle,* for you are the fewest of any people, *nomadic or otherwise, and obviously, the easiest and the dumbest backward population to swiftly influence, infiltrate and obliterate.*

But because the Lord hath *inexplicably* loved you *in His mysterious non-sexual way,* and hath kept His oath *about you low-mentality oafs,* which He swore to your *three main sperm-rich fathers, now all deceased:* and hath brought you out *of King Pharaoh's Egypt* with a *Royal Flush* strong hand, and *commendably* redeemed you from the *sadistic* house of bondage, out of the hand of the *anonymous no-name* Pharaoh, the *non-nostalgic undistinguished* King of Egypt *without a first, middle or last name.*

And thou shalt know that the Lord thy God; He is a strong and faithful God *and therefore, does not have to exercise in any gym or health spa in either Holy Heaven or on Contaminated Earth,* keeping

His covenant and mercy to them (*folks*) that love Him, and to them that keep His Commandments *locked-up in safes, in strong boxes and in remote safety deposit boxes,* unto a thousand generations *multiplied to the third power.*

And repaying forthwith them that hate Him for other reasons *besides His bitter envy, jealousy and propensity for massive revenge,* so as to destroy them *(the spiteful pagans) into minuscule dust particles,* without further delay, immediately rendering to them what they deserve: *castration, bowel removal, suffocation, all followed by high-heat incineration and by convection stove cremation too.*

Keep therefore the precepts, *forceps* and ceremonies and judgments, which I command thee this day to do, *or else pay with your lives the dire consequences already specifically defined here in the magnificent Wholly Book of Doo-Doo-Rot-on-Me.*

If after thou hast heard these *fairly harsh Draconian* judgments, thou keep and do them *if you value your necessary assholes,* and the Lord thy God will also maintain His covenant to thee *by allowing you to keep on living, farting and taking relieving shits normally,* and the mercy which He *solemnly* swore to thy fathers *shall be maintained, and thus, you will be able to keep your undesirable pauper status for many years and decadent decades.*

And He will love thee and multiply thee *by using the newly developed arithmetic times table chart,* and will bless the fruit *and vegetables* of thy womb, and the fruit, *nuts and testicles* of all thy land, thy corn, *corns, warts, wens and calluses too,* and thy vintage, thy oil, *thy oily skin, thy pimples and acne,* and thy herds, and the flocks of thy *bleating bleeding* sheep upon the land, for which He swore to thy *three principal sperm-laden deceased non-triplet* fathers that He would give it thee.

Blessed shalt thou be among all people, *for the rest don't give a silent shit about my prerequisite religious message, especially the pagan pedophiles, the pagan prostitutes, the pagan assholes and all the other non-Hebrew pagan jerk-offs flourishing all over the Known World, which, to my inferior knowledge, is very limited in scope and size.* No one shall be barren among you of either sex, neither of men nor cattle. *Not even those among you without genitals will be barren.*

43

And even the cattle without genitals will be just as fertile as the land that the itinerant herds relentlessly bullshit upon.

The Lord will take away from thee all sickness *and bothersome venereal diseases:* and the grievous infirmities of Pagan Egypt, which thou knowest *as HIV, HIVES, AIDS, and other similar medical phenomenon accursed-type bullshit.* He will not bring upon thee, but upon thy *immoral* enemies, *especially the dumb-ass pagan men who stick their erect dicks into crowded beehives and wasp nests!*

Thou shalt consume all the people *without ever practicing the art of cannibalism, all of* which the Lord thy God will *conveniently* deliver to thee *and thy doorstep, that is, if you're luckily living in a portable house, sturdy donkey cart or hole-less tent.* Thy eye, *thy pupils, and thy students* shall not spare them, neither shalt thou serve their gods, lest they be thy ruin *if you wish to feel and be devastated.*

If thou *Israel* say in thy heart *with thy heart's tongue, larynx and throat, all coordinated and synchronized:* "These nations are more than I; how shall I be able to destroy them *if dynamite and atomic bombs have never been invented?"*

Fear not *Hebrew Doubters,* but remember what the Lord thy God did to the *anonymous* Pharaoh and to all the *rambunctious* Egyptians, *those smelly-assed fools who have had chronic diarrhea twenty-four hours a day for two whole years now. If you recall, they also have hearing AIDS from doing perverted sex.*

The exceeding great plagues, which thy eyes saw *and amply appreciated,* and the *various billboard* signs and *Biblical advertising* wonders, and the strong *Heavenly* hand *that allowed you to finally get a grip,* and the *sensational* stretched-out *elastic* arm *from the floating clouds,* with which the Lord thy God brought thee out *of an archangel's magician top hat:* so will He do to all the *strange* people, whom thou now fearest. *Those sinning pagan charlatans will ultimately be defeated and converted, just like certain kinds of rice. Just ask Benjamin's Uncle Ben about this shit.*

Moreover the Lord thy God will send also hornets among them, *and strange humans known as White Anglo-Saxon Protestants too will have bees in their bonnets* until He destroys and consumes all that have escaped thee, (along with the many *infidels* who call themselves *pagans),* because the Lord thy God is in the midst of thee, a God mighty and terrible, *Who despises mighty and puny sinners alike, pornography wall drawers, homosexuals, sodomists, lesbians, bisexuals and ultra-terrifying trans-gender transvestites.*

He has a lot on His plate and will consume these *aberrant* nations in thy sight, little and little, and by *Bachelor and Masters'* degrees *also.* Thou wilt not be able to destroy them altogether *all at once:* lest perhaps the beasts of the Earth should increase upon thee *and we males all will then become Beastly Boys.*

But the Lord thy God shall deliver them in thy sight *and onto your irises and retinas:* and shall slay them until they be utterly destroyed and *immediately turned into greasy offal.* And He shall deliver their kings, *queens, aces and jacks* into thy *poker and pee-knuckle* hands, and thou shalt destroy their names *and I.D.'s* from under Heaven: no man shall be able to resist thee, until thou destroy them, *even without the aid of yet-to-be-invented dynamite and atomic bombs.*

Their graven things thou shalt burn with fire and brimstone: *throw the brazen images (along with the pagan violators) into the craters of active erupting volcanoes!* Thou shalt not covet the silver and gold of which they *(the false gods)* are made; *Say to yourself: Their mines are not mine!* Neither shalt thou take to thee anything thereof, lest thou *wickedly* offend *our entire religious on-the-lam traveling crusade,* because it is an abomination to the Lord thy God *to steal from lowlife poor pagans.*

Graven things... fucked-up Idols, so called by contempt. Neither shalt thou bring any thing of the idol into thy house, lest thou become a *fucked-up idle* anathema, *just like it is. There is nothing worse than an idle idol aimlessly standing like an idiotic immobile statue on your splintery breakfast table.* Thou shalt detest it as *elephant, horse or donkey* dung, *and if Levi does not offer you dungarees to wear while curiously staring at the abominable idle idol, then* you shalt utterly abhor it as uncleanness and filth, because it is an anathema *and is an absolute disgrace and shame to all that is*

Wholly Holy if we even dare to worship dung wearing Levi dungarees.

Chapter Eight

"God's Care"

Until we have social welfare programs like Medicare, we Israelites will have to cope with God's Care. The people are put in mind of God's *wheelings and* dealings with them *and their fate,* to the end that they may love Him and serve Him *as His obedient robotic servants, and not as independent educated self-dignified human beings.*

All the Commandments, that I command thee this *cold miserable* day, *and that none of you apathetic clowns apparently give a flying shit about,* take great care to observe *this overly repetitious statement:* that you may live, and be multiplied, and going *into coveted alien territories* may *greedily* possess the *desired* land, for which the Lord swore to your *three* fathers *would be easily pilfered and obtained.*

And thou shalt remember all the way through which the Lord thy God hath brought thee for forty years through the *unnamed barren* desert, *even without a horse with no name,* to afflict thee *and to immensely piss you off,* and to prove thee and *suffer thee, without making thy more vociferous women into rabid radical suffragettes,* and that the things that were known in thy heart might be *also* made known *in thy brain,* whether thou wouldst keep His Commandments or not. *But this learning process cannot be accomplished until we actually realize that the brain and the heart are separate body organs having quite different biological functions.*

He afflicted thee with want *and wont,* and gave thee manna *manana and today* for thy food, which neither thou nor thy fathers knew *shit about because they were not well-bred about making and baking bread:* to show that not in bread alone doth *Hebrew* man live, but in every word that proceedeth from the mouth of God *to satisfy our basic bagel kneads with His seemingly half-baked ideas. Just ask Reuben who will gladly tell you that a sandwich is indeed more than bread alone to live by!*

Not in bread alone, etc... That is, that God is able to make food of what He *so* pleases for the support of *Hebrew* man, *who has yet to learn how to put either round or square holes in doughnuts.*

Thy raiment *and rags,* with which thou wast covered, hath not decayed for age, *even though most of the men now have moth balls after dis-robing,* and thy foot is not worn, *since obviously it is attached to the body and is not clothing;* lo, this is the fortieth year *and we still haven't gone from rags to riches, or even from rags to religious socialism.*

That thou mayst consider in thy heart, that as a man traineth up his son *like a pet dog or horse is traineth up,* so the Lord thy God hath trained thee up *to piss and crap in stenchy window-less outhouses.* That thou shouldst keep the Commandments of the Lord thy God, and walk in His ways, and fear Him is *how I plan to control your random fucked-up relentless misconduct.* For the Lord thy God will *surely* bring thee into a *goodie-goodie fantasy* land, of *wondrous* brooks and of waters, and of *water-slides and diving boards that don't dive,* and of fountains *and imaginary fountain pens:* in the plains of which and where the hills' deep rivers break-out *like teenage acne and adult skin and venereal disease rashes.*

A land of wheat, and barley, and vineyards, wherein fig trees and pomegranates, and olive-yards grow *like thick dense jungles:* a land of oil and honey, *and we shall enjoy this stolen land without any fraudulent milk or fake imitation honey, until the cows come home or until the bees learn simple basic geography! A marvelous land* where without any want *or wont,* thou shalt eat thy bread *and enjoy it like leven-worth,* and *also* enjoy abundance of all things *of which I can't fuckin' remember right now:* where the stones are *round* iron, and out of its hills are dug mines of *huge* brass *balls for our soldiers to proudly wear, always exposed and frightfully bouncing-around to the enemy's eyes.*

That when thou hast eaten *voraciously of the savory stolen food,* and art full *of intestinal gas from your skinny rectums right up to your corpulent stomachs,* thou mayst bless the Lord thy God for the excellent land which He hath *generously* given thee, *all for free from the invaded idol-worshiping ambitious pagans.*

Take heed *mercurial Israelites,* and beware *of sin and the gross evils of bodily pleasure,* lest at any time thou *impulsively* forget the Lord thy God *for a repugnant quicky piece of ass,* and neglect His *inflexible* Commandments and judgments and ceremonies, which I command thee *on* this *cold miserable* day to *obediently* follow *while spontaneously abandoning sex, fellatio and fellow-atio with other perverted men.*

Lest after thou hast eaten and art filled *with abundant gaseous fecal matter,* hast built goodly-*goodly two-shoes pebble houses,* and dwelt in them *during massive earthquakes to test their flimsy durability.* And thou shalt have *hordes of* herds of *hoarded* oxen and flocks of sheep, and plenty of gold and of silver, and of all things *too, so that you un-illustrious morons can fully understand the lexicography of cute linguistic Hebrew oxymorons.*

Thy heart be lifted-up *without the aid of adroit cardiologists,* and thou remember not the Lord thy God *from geriatric memory loss, the Great Spirit* Who brought thee out of the land of Egypt, out of the *dreaded S and M* house of bondage located there.

And was thy leader in the great and terrible *wild* wilderness, wherein there was the serpent burning with his *vile halitosis* breath, and the *sting-operation* scorpion and the *Dip-shit* Dipsas, and no waters at all *to deliberately drown-in:* Who *amazingly had in His genius* brought forth streams out of the hardest rock *cafes belonging to the industrious and conscientious pagan natives.*

The *vicious Dip-shit* Dipsas... A *desert* serpent whose bite causeth a violent thirst; so the serpent must bite again and again *to extract more liquid blood from your veins and arteries to quench his mighty fluid needs;* from whence it has its name, for in Greek 'dipsa' signifies thirst, and *Dip-shit Dipsas signifies that you will be sucked-clean of liquid until only hard and soft shit remains inside your cruddy disintegrating bowels.*

And *He* fed thee in the wilderness with manna which thy *three* fathers knew not *because the freakin' assholes were all on gluten-free diets without ever even having any indication of sprue disease.* And after He had afflicted and proved thee *just to demonstrate His awesome power and to assess your capacity for coping with torment,* at the last He had mercy on thee *after your pained uncles finally yelled-out "Father!" while admitting experiencing defeat.*

Lest thou shouldst *selfishly* say in thy *tongue-less* heart: "My own might, and the strength of my own hand have achieved all these things for me, *for I use all four chambers in my heart but yet only one hand (the right one, I think) to accomplish and perform my everyday mundane survival tasks.*

But remember the Lord thy God, that He hath given you *your* strength, *even to you hateful ninety pound beach weaklings,* that He might fulfill His *sacred* covenant, concerning which He swore to thy three *ancestral* fathers, *who were not identical triplets, but fathers of each other from three distinct generations,* as this present day *religious experiment* sheweth.

But if thou forget the *unforgettable* Lord thy God, and follow strange gods *all over creation, queer gay gods who magically turn from statues into faggot walking animal forms,* and serve them *tennis balls* and adore them *as if they're naked big-breasted women:* behold now I foretell thee that thou shalt utterly perish *and luckily depart the evil Earth and fortunately escape through sudden death His continuous relentless wrath.*

As the nations, which the Lord destroyed at thy entrance *into this oddball Biblical Side Show called Deuteronomy,* so shall you also perish *like perishable diseased fruit,* if you be disobedient to the Voice of the Lord your God, *Who incidentally never gets laryngitis, but Who kicks Hebrew and pagan butt quite religiously.*

Chapter Nine

"Unmerited Success"

Lest they *(sinners, the Israelites; a definite pronoun-antecedent problem existing here with no indicative noun antecedent given)* should impute their victories to their own merits, they are put in mind of their manifold rebellions *against the Commandments* and other *prominent* sins, for which they should have been destroyed *and promptly emulsified and vaporized,* but God spared them for His *huge* promise made to Abraham, Isaac, and Jacob, *which was not to swiftly terminate or exterminate too many of their asshole loony descendants.*

Hear, O Israel: Thou shalt go over the Jordan this day *without a boat, dingy, canoe, ark, cruise ship or a raft;* to possess nations very great, and stronger than thyself, *nations with dazzling* cities having *infra-red infrastructure, having metropolitan downtown shopping areas and having clean market places,* great *architecture, functional rest rooms* and *the urban area being* walled-up to the *clear blue* sky.

A people great and tall, *enjoying excellent high protein diets,* the sons of the *bastard* Enacims and the s*ons-of-bitches who are detestable Enacims too,* whom Thou hast seen, and heard of, against whom no man is able to stand, *for the whole lot of the awesome Enacim enemy is obnoxious and rather deficient in personality.*

Thou shalt know therefore this day that the Lord thy God Himself will pass over before thee, *moving as fast as a flashing lightning bolt,* a devouring and consuming fire *that might electrocute any gullible unwary human witness,* to destroy and extirpate and bring them to nothing before thy face quickly, as He hath spoken to thee, *but only I Moses had heard His threatening enigmatic words.*

Say not in thy *talking* heart, when the Lord thy God shall have destroyed them in thy sight, *a scene worse than Sodom and Gomorrah after their well-deserved dual destruction:* For my justice hath the Lord brought me in to possess this *incredibly infertile* land, whereas these nations are destroyed for their wickedness, *and we are subsequently rewarded for our persistent prodigious greediness.*

For it is not for thy *questionable* justices, *Archangels' Gabriel and Michael who sit on the Lord's Supreme Court,* and the uprightness of thy heart that thou shalt go in to possess their *(the pagans) personal* lands: but because they have done wickedly, they are destroyed at thy coming in *encroachment and blitz:* and that the Lord might accomplish His *favorite* word *"Destroy,"* which He promised by oath to thy *numbskull* fathers Abraham, Isaac, and Jacob, *none of whom gave a half-shit then about anything, and all of whom don't give a minuscule shit now about anything because the three Hebrew patriarchs are indisputably stone cold morbidly dead.*

Know therefore that the Lord thy God giveth thee not this excellent land in possession for thy justices, for thou art a very stiff-necked people, *and stiff-dicked and occasionally stiff-titted too.* Remember, and forget not how thou provokedst the Lord thy God to *monumental* wrath in the *desert* wilderness, *making you drink prune juice twenty-four hours a day for two whole consecutive years.* From the day that thou camest out of Egypt unto this *forsaken desert* place, thou hast always strove against the Lord, *greatly pissing both Him and me (Moses) off while you imitate and impersonate the fucked-up happy-go-lucky pagans.*

For in Horeb, at the base of the *magic* mountain, also thou didst provoke Him by *disrespectfully* ignoring His Ten Laws, and He was angry *as all Hell at your despicable defiance,* and would have destroyed thee, *for all we had to do according to His prescribed instructions was to take His two tablets, go to sleep and then see Him in the morning.*

When I went up into the mount *(and not upon it)* to receive the *burdensome* tables of stone, the tables of the covenant which the Lord made with you *out of rare salt and basalt:* and I continued in the mount forty days and nights, neither eating bread, nor drinking water, *wishing the entire time that I would fuckin' instantly die and end it all.*

And the Lord gave me two tables of stone *exclusively* written with the *inky* finger of God, and containing all the words that He spoke to you in the mount from the midst of the *furious* fire, when the *Israelite* people were assembled together, *the foolish journeymen trying to piss the Lord's symbolic fire out with their yard-long erect peckers, which were in danger of being incinerated in a giant community sausage roast.*

And when forty days were passed, and as many nights *and weeks too,* the Lord gave me the two tables of stone, the tables of the covenant, *which frankly I didn't know how to read or interpret.* And *He* said to me: "Arise *Fool Moses,* and go down from hence quickly: for thy people, which thou hast brought out of Egypt *where they were quite happier living as slaves,* have quickly forsaken the way that thou hast shewn them, and have made to themselves a molten idol *comprised of active volcanic lava.*

And again the Lord said to me: "I see that this people *you have led here from Egypt* happen to be stiff-necked *and stiff-dicked, even when they piss-out My intense fire flames.* Let Me alone, *so* that I may destroy them *with lethal urine from the dark clouds,* and abolish their name from under Heaven, *since they only have one single first and last name amongst them all,* and set thee over a nation, that is greater and stronger than this *clumsy rabble. For Moses, I think we'd have better luck converting the arrogant pagans to obeying My Ten Commandments and then having the crazed apostates worship Me.*

And when I came down from the burning mount *(actually, only the tiny bush was ablaze, a small bush no bigger than a woman's),* and I held the two tables of the covenant with both hands, *for they had weighed three hundred pounds each.* And I saw that you had sinned against the Lord your God, and had made to yourselves a molten calf *with frightful volcanic ash and lava flowing out of its fat ass and tiny dick respectively,* and had quickly forsaken His way, which He had shewn you, *that the only suitable solution would be to have the Israelites' exposed assholes immediately cauterized with a flurry of electrifying lightning bolts speeding directly up your tender rectums.*

I cast the tables out of my hands, and broke them in your sight, *for in truth I had been just as stoned as the three hundred pound tablets.* And *next I stumbled over a branch and* fell down before the Lord as before, forty days and nights, neither eating bread, nor drinking water, *to atone* for all your sins, *but despite my great spectacular effort, I still was unable to successfully commit a decent suicide. But still,* you had committed *egregious sin and corruption* against the Lord, *and like immature kindergarten children,* had provoked Him to wrath *against you, making Him act like an affronted first grader.*

For I feared His *tremendous* indignation and anger, *although the rest of you low-brows just didn't give a proletarian shit,* wherewith being moved against you, He would have destroyed you *if I hadn't stupidly interceded on your behalf.* And the Lord heard me this time also, *my mouth foolishly acting as your quixotic defense attorney.*

And He was exceeding angry against Aaron also, and would have destroyed Him *by pulling a hair hank out of Aaron's scalp,* and I prayed in like manner for him, *my younger brother, who I think lived before the time of Homer.*

And your sin that you had committed, that is, worshiping the molten calf *with the volcanic ash and lava shooting out of its fat ass and tiny dick respectively,* and then, I took, and ignited it with fire, getting third degree burns all over my *vulnerable* torso *from the series of terrible chemical explosions that had unexpectedly erupted,* and breaking it into pieces, until the idol was as small as dust, I threw it into the torrent, which cometh down from the mountain. *All this remarkable bullshit was happening while my scorched hands were still smoldering and shooting-out a flurry of flesh embers.*

At the *calf idol* burning also, and at the place of temptation, and at the graves of lust, you had provoked the Lord. *I then noticed that my own friggin' calves were on fire, and thus using my mental guile, I extinguished the two lower leg fires by smartly leaping into the adjacent river.*

And when He sent you from *the crummy malodorous barns* at Cadesbarne, saying: "Go up, and possess the land that I have given you, and you slighted the Commandment of the Lord your God, and did not believe Him, neither would you hearken to His voice, *foolishly arguing all-the-while that this new Commandment had not been written on the original stone tablets with the first ten directives.*

But *you confederates* were always rebellious from the day that I began to know you *back at the notorious Egyptian S and M Bondage House along the Nile.* And I *again* lay prostrate *on my prostate* before the Lord forty days and nights, in which I humbly besought Him, that He would not destroy you as He had *indignantly* threatened. *But despite my valiant forty day fasting, which honestly went by very slowly, I was not able to die as I had sincerely wanted to do.*

And praying, I said: "O Lord God, destroy not Thy *sinful* people, and Thy inheritance *too,* which Thou hast redeemed in Thy greatness, whom Thou hast brought out of Egypt with a strong hand *that had already beaten four Kings of Diamonds.* Remember Thy dead servants Abraham, Isaac, and Jacob: look not on the stubbornness of this *idol-worshiping* people, nor on their wickedness and sin. *I mean Lord, it wasn't my damned fault that each of them (the recalcitrant and incorrigible Israelites) was born with a stubbed head!*

Lest perhaps the inhabitants of the *pagan* land, out of which Thou hast brought us, say: "The Lord could not bring them into the land that He promised them, and He hated them: therefore He brought them out, that He might kill them in the wilderness." *'But Lord,' I thought and evaluated, 'I don't think the neighborhood pagans give a crap about that irrelevant Ten Commandment nonsense either! The nutcase Israelites* are Thy people and Thy inheritance, whom Thou hast brought out by Thy great *supernatural* strength, and in Thy stretched-out *unbelievable elastic* arm *too.'* *"Now Lord," I futilely exclaimed to the ear-less Heavens, "why the hell can't I commit a standard-type commonplace suicide?"*

Chapter Ten

"New Stones and a Wooden Ark"

The Divine Omnipotent Spirit had told me (Moses) in a recent disturbing dream that Chapter Ten was much better than Chapter Eleven, whatever the hell those obscure enigmatic words had meant. But then in that same weird manifestation God *the Almighty* giveth *me* the second tables of the law: a further exhortation to fear and serve the Lord, *and also, a second reason why the 'don't give a shit' Israelites should follow my suspect leadership. Listen-up Assholes, before it is too late!*

At that *chaotic* time *in prehistoric history* the Lord said to me *while I had been preoccupied collecting edible scorpions somewhere out in the arid desert: "Here!* Hew thee two tables of stone like the former ones *you had angrily smashed into smithereens. I want to see Moses if you can actually cut it or not! You might even institute my Bureau of Engraving and Printing! And then* come up to Me' into the mount: and thou shalt make an ark of wood *devoid of ravenous termites. This new wooden ark shall be an ark-eological phenomenon if ever discovered in the distant future by baffled exploring idiots looking for Noah's ship!"*

And I will *be inspired to* write upon the tables the words that were in them *(the original tablets),* which thou *you clumsy klutz, without My expressed permission or consent,* brokest before, and thou shalt *as a special assignment* put them *(the shattered stone bits and pieces)* inside *the wooden* ark, *which shall be then called, for lack of better terminology, the Ark of the Covenant.*

And me being a retired craftsman/carpenter in search of an appropriate retirement avocation, I made an ark of setim wood *completely devoid of nasty carpenter ants and voracious termites.* And when I had hewn two tables of stone like the former *ones I had violently shattered,* I *laboriously struggled* and went up into the mount, having them *(the new tablets)* in my hands, *each one weighing exactly three-hundred pounds, just like the old ones before.*

And He wrote *(scribbled) some unsophisticated nomenclature* in the tables, *according to* as He had written before, the ten words *that*

57

were really short imperative sentences, but certainly not a cohesive paragraph, which the Lord spoke to you in the mount from the midst of the *blazing bush and brush* fire, when the *lazy* people were assembled, *expecting something much more spectacular and pleasure-oriented than two ordinary-looking dictatorial stone tablets:* and He gave them to me as a form of spiritual welfare *without any accompanying food or manna stamps.*

And *then* returning from the *steep and precarious* mount *precipice,* I came, *slid and then tumbled* down, and *next I* put the *stone* tables into the *center of the wooden* ark, *symbolizing that we the inferior Israelites were finally emerging from the primitive Stone Age; yes,* the stone tablets and the wooden ark that I had made, and they are there *as the main exhibits in an open-air museum* till this present, as the *incomprehensible* Lord *had despotically* commanded me *to perform as a subordinate puppet existing upon His unfathomable Stage of Life.*

And the children of Israel *(You didn't know that the country had a uterus, did you?)* removed their camp from Beroth *Obama,* of the children of Jacan into Mosera, *the mysterious place* where *my brother* Aaron had died and was buried *somewhere in the infamous city dump, where the constipated residents all took daily dumps,* and Eleazar his *(Brother Aaron's)* son succeeded him in the priestly office, *honorably serving as Chief Area Pedophile Administrator.*

Mosera... by Mount Hor, *situated next to Mount Prostitute and across from Mount Harlot,* for there Aaron had died, *as validly recorded and reported in* Numbers: 20. This and the following verses seem to be inserted by way of parenthesis, *a sort of meaningless and inconsequential parenthetical expression, I feel quite compelled to indicate and orally record.*

From thence they came to Gadgad, *not too far from Dad-Dad,* from which place they *soon* departed, *so the indolent wanderers were always walking around in redundant concentric circles all over the hot damned desert sands. And finally, the aimless direction-less trekkers* camped in Jetebatha, in a land of waters, *water slide parks, boardwalks* and *horrendous* torrents, *situated near Glad-Glad, an extremely evil lesbian and gay oasis.*

58

At that time He separated the tribe of Levi, to carry the ark of the covenant of the Lord *wearing their tight denim dungarees,* and to stand before Him in the ministry, and to bless in his name until this present day *when their blue canvas uniforms were supposed to colorfully turn to a bright red fabric, but never did. To tell the truth, deep-down inside, the independent-minded obdurate Levis were not entirely dye-in-the-wool religious zealots.*

Wherefore Levi' *in his denim jeans* hath no part nor possession with his brethren: because the Lord Himself is his possession, as the Lord thy God promised him *at the Gap situated between Mount Hor and Mount Harlot.*

And I stood in the mount *rather than upon it, and just as several times* before, forty days and nights *I stood there like a motionless zombie statue:* and the Lord heard me *prattling and ranting away,* this time *in that remote inhospitable solitude* also, and *I must tell you that* the Lord would not destroy thee *either because He happened to be in a rare good mood that pleasant day.*

And recognizing that I was both delirious and delusional from forty days and forty nights of severe starvation, He said to me: "Go Moses, and walk before the people *on the boardwalk promenade situated next to the closed-for-the-summer water slide park,* that they *(the nomadic Israelites)* may enter *without paying cheap admission,* and possess the *soon-to-be-acquired (confiscated)* land, which I swore to their fathers that I would give them *after they have stolen it from the uncooperative and sinful pagan natives.*

And now, Israel, what doth the Lord thy God require of thee *incompetent listless boobs,* but that thou fear the Lord thy God, and walk in His ways *but not in His way,* and love Him *because you obviously fear Him,* and serve the Lord thy God *despite the fact that we have no metal or wooden trays in which to serve anybody; serve Him* with all thy heart, and with all thy soul, *and with unquestioned loyal blind obedience. Yes, I insist that you dunces serve Him soul food from thy hearts; otherwise risk being blinded.*

And if you at all value your dispensable lives and also your vulnerable scrawny rear ends, keep the Ten Commandments of the Lord, and His ceremonies, *along with His rites and Last Rites,* which

I command thee this day, *although I lack unnecessary authority and permission from you silly incapable assholes,* that it may be well with thee? *And whatever you do, you' dunce-headed Israelites, don't ever break His stones like I had done! You'll too have to starve against your will for forty days and forty nights as I had been cruelly forced to do! Believe me you insolent Doubting Dolts; disobedience to the strict Ten Commandments engraved on stone just isn't fuckin' worth it! And quite succinctly, don't tumble the tablets down any high mountain because rolling stones gather no moss!*

Behold Heaven is the Lord's thy God, and the Heaven of heavens, the Earth and all things that are therein. *So in my humble limited estimation, enjoy and appreciate Earth while we live, because resplendent Heaven is no doubt unattainable to us unqualified hapless mortals. Paradise is the exclusive domain of the all-powerful privileged Lord, and it is home to no one else!*

And yet the Lord hath been closely *and chauvinistically* joined to thy fathers, *but not to thy mothers, sisters, nieces, grandmothers and aunts,* and He loved them *(thy three deceased fathers)* and chose their seed *to plant into horny women* after them, that is to say, you, out of all nations, as this day it *(the wonderful practice)* is *quite questionably* proved.

Circumcise therefore the foreskin of your heart, and stiffen your neck no more. Therefore, let your hearts ejaculate truth, *if your hearts can symbolically maintain decent erections! And by all means, feed your removed heart and dick foreskins to the hungry desert dogs and predatory jackals! It's no skin off your backs, but at least you will have some skin in the game!*

Listen to my worthy words, you mindless Imbeciles assembled here in the formidable desert heat! Because the Lord your God He is the God of gods, and the Lord of lords, a great God and mighty and terrible, Who accepteth no person nor taketh bribes. *Fear Him more than earthquakes, floods, comets, meteors, asteroids, hemorrhoids, fire and brimstone, typhoons and monsoons, volcano eruptions and last but not least, monstrous tsunamis.*

He doth judgment to the fatherless and the widow, *and the dreaded African black widow too, and He* loveth the stranger, and giveth him food and raiment *(garments), that is to say, to all strangers (potential converts) who are not native pagans.*

And do you therefore love strangers, *both gay male and lesbian female,* because you also were strangers in the land of Egypt. *I fully realize that you apathetic Idiots do not fathom complicated philosophical rhetorical questions, so why the fuck am I wasting my precious time lecturing and pandering to you!*

For the thousandth time, thou shalt fear the Lord thy God, and serve Him only: *I warn you all for the last fuckin' time: don't work in any restaurants or pizza shops, and whatever you do, don't wait on tables!* Serve only the Lord! To Him thou shalt adhere, and shalt swear by His name. *On second thought, don't ever swear His name if you sincerely value your life, your balls, your flabby tits and your vulnerable asshole! Why put your very existence into an unnecessary existential crisis?*

And for the millionth time, He is thy praise, and thy God, Who hath done for thee these great and terrible things, *like giving you stone tablets and a wooden ark,* which thy *bloodshot and fatigued* eyes have seen *and intentionally ignored.*

In seventy souls thy fathers went down into Egypt *in search of their kindred soul brothers:* and behold now the Lord thy God hath multiplied thee as the stars of Heaven: *despite my garrulous bullshitting prattle, in relation to Earth, you just have to believe that He had to 'plan it' that way!*

Chapter Eleven

"The Wonders of the Lord"

The love and service of God are still inculcated, with a blessing to them *(only me)* that serve Him, and threats of punishment if they *(the unreliable Israelites)* forsake His law *and declare Chapter Eleven even before I write the damned thing. Abide by and heed these imperative teachings and not be morally bankrupt.*

Therefore, *and how many times must I repeat this urgent message,* love the Lord thy God and observe His *extraordinary* precepts and ceremonies, His *incomprehensible* judgments and Commandments at all times *or else your rectum and your colon along with your targeted semi-colon will be painfully cauterized.*

Know this day the things that your children *without calendars* know not, who saw not the *horrific* chastisements of the Lord your God, His great doings and strong hand, and stretched-out *elastic* arm *that I suspect might be partially made of thin rubber.*

The signs and works *(Interpretation: destruction and devastation)* which He did in the midst of Egypt to King Pharaoh, and to all His land, *causing great suffering, misery, constipation and contagious diarrhea among the afflicted population.*

And to all the host *and hostesses* of the Egyptians, and to their horses and chariots *and various clever pyramid schemes:* how the waters of the Red Sea covered them *before and after their doomed soldiers had spontaneously drowned,* when they pursued you *without wearing inflatable safety jackets,* and how the Lord destroyed them *and their modern souped-up chariots,* until this present day, *remember our phenomenal victory.*

And what He hath done to you in the wilderness, till you came to this *horrendous barren* place: And to Dathan and Abiron, the *nauseating* sons of Eliab, who was the son of Reuben, *the deli-sandwich man:* whom the Earth, opening her mouth swallowed-up with their households and tents, and all their substance, which they had in the midst of Israel, *gone and eradicated forever, instantaneously disappearing into a gigantic prehistoric sink-hole, not even having Pharaoh's faucet in the sink.*

Your eyes have seen all the great works of the Lord, that He hath done, and yet you *offensive* Israelites *don't give a rat's ass after being thoroughly illuminated like human fire-flies, all done by the one and only Lord thy God.*

All the fantastic deeds wondrously performed so that you may keep all His Commandments, which I command you to do *out of sheer fear of reprisal* this day, and may go in, and possess the *well-defended* land, to which you are entering, *and to which we shall get our punk butts brutally kicked, just for boldly attempting to commit grand larceny against the obstinate ruthless pagans.*

And may live in it a long time *as injured hospital patients with our wounded legs, dicks and tits in traction: land* which the Lord promised by oath to your *non-triplet inattentive* fathers, and to their seed, a land which floweth with milk and honey, *for even seeds masquerading as sperms enjoy being recognized and talked to from time to time.*

For the land, which *(for the ten millionth time)* thou goest to possess, is not like the land of Egypt, from whence thou camest out, where, when the seed is sown *into a lady's wet pink vagina,* waters are brought in to dampen it after the manner of *flourishing* gardens. *So for example, if your wife's name is 'Mary', as the popular saying goes, "Mary, Mary, quite contrary, how does your' furry garden grow?"*

But it is a land of hills and plains, *and plain hills and hilly plains,* all expecting rain from Heaven, *for hills and plains can think, anticipate and expect things like a surprise rain too.* And the Lord thy God doth always visit it *(the plain hills and the hilly plains),* and His eyes are on it from the beginning of the year unto the end thereof, *diligently circling each important date on a calendar chart that He had borrowed from His celestial Olympus mountain friend Zeus.*

If then you obey my Commandments, *which are really His Commandments, resilient laws* which I command you *to obey* this

64

very day, that you love the Lord your God, and serve Him with all your heart, and with all your soul: *but I hereby caution you self-serving Fools, don't expect Him to either love you or serve you in return!*

He will give to your land the early rain and the latter rain, that you may gather in your' corn, and your wine, and your oil, *for April showers bring May-flowers, as the future pilgrims to Utopian America will certainly discover. And the short rainfalls will not be ridiculously called Baby Showers!*

And your hay out of the fields to feed your cattle, and that you may eat and be filled, *so Assholes, I advise that you make hay while the sun shines, or else you Hillbilly Hicks, you might never have a happy hey-day to enjoy.*

Beware lest perhaps your heart *(the whole million of you' retarded losers have only one small heart to share)* be deceived, and you depart from the Lord, and *egregiously* serve strange gods, and adore them *along with their fascinating shooting-lava erect penises and the insidious idols' molten rock-firing assholes.*

And the Lord being angry shut-up Heaven, that the rain came not down, *but instead exits the atmosphere and waters the moon, dropping torrents and deluge in the opposite direction of everything else;* nor the Earth yield *her sweet and bittersweet* fruit, and you shall perish quickly from the excellent land, which the Lord will give you *on a probationary basis. So you smart-assed Deviates', I strongly advise that you don't deviate from honoring the Ten Commandments.*

Lay up these words in your hearts and minds, and hang them for a sign on your hands, and place them between your eyes, *and then perhaps your hands will get shingles from the exhibited shingles.* Teach your children that they meditate *for hours, days, months and years* on them *(the Ten Commandments),* when thou sittest in thy house, and when thou walkest on the way *to a local beer garden or thriving brothel,* and when thou liest-down and risest-up *before and during (but not after) sex.*

Thou shalt write them *(the Ten Commandments)* upon the posts and the doors of thy house, *for that method does not constitute graffiti when solely done to your own slum home.*

That thy days may be multiplied *by the highest common denominator available,* and that the days of thy children in the land which the Lord swore to thy *three lackadaisical* fathers, that He would give them *as long to figure-out what the hell to do as the majestic Heaven hangeth over the baneful Earth.*

For if you *faithfully* and *loyally* keep the Commandments which I command you, and do them, to love the Lord your God, and walk in all His ways, cleaving unto Him, *I predict that you will still go nowhere (except into the ground) when you die.*

For lack of anything better to do, and out of sheer boredom, the Lord will *mercilessly* destroy all these nations before your face *(faces),* and you shall possess them *(both the conquered nations and your faces),* which are greater and stronger than you, *but nevertheless, have surrendered without respectable resistance to a pack of total wimps.*

Every place, that your' foot *(feet)* shall tread upon, shall be yours, *even your contaminating carbon footprints.* From the desert, and from Libanus, from the great river Euphrates unto the western sea shall be your borders, *so just play the Lord's avaricious conquest game in-bounds and not out-of-bounds.*

None shall stand against you: the Lord your God shall lay the dread and fear of you upon all the land that you shall tread upon, as He hath spoken to you. *For those two emotional abstractions are His basic valued themes: "Dread and fear!"*

Behold *Breathing Brethren,* I *now* set forth in your sight this day *both* a blessing and a curse. A blessing, if you obey the Commandments of the Lord your God, which I command you this day. *Don't fuckin' obey the stern edicts and you might wind-up becoming and being the next me!* And *as far as* a curse *is concerned,* if you obey not the Commandments of the Lord your God, but revolt from the way which now I show you, and walk after strange *lava-*

assed gods with *molten squirting penises and fire-farting assholes,* which you know not.

And when the Lord thy God shall have brought thee into the land *(for the umpteenth time),* whither thou goest to dwell, thou shalt put the blessing upon Mount Garizim, the curse upon Mount Hebal, *and then humbly count your blessings and tabulate your curses.*

All of the above which are beyond the Jordan, behind the way that goeth to the setting of the sun, *a western sunset being a terrific setting,* in the land of the Canaanite who dwelleth in the plain country over against Galgala, which is near the valley that reacheth and entereth far, *near the infamous Gal-gal-a Gala Whorehouse and the equally popular Adjunct Pagan Sexual Aids Museum.*

For you shall *clandestinely* pass over the Jordan *riding upon the backs of submerged donkeys, your assigned purpose being* to possess the land, which the Lord your God will give you, that you may have it and possess it. *But watch-out my chosen Brethren because the shrewd pagan inhabitants' might be veteran Re-Po men' in disguise.*

See therefore that you fulfill the *prescribed* ceremonies and judgments, which I shall set this day before you, *or else join the mendacious pagan league and die in swarms like countless poisoned flitting fruit flies.*

Chapter Twelve

"The Sanctuary"

All idolatry must be extirpated *if you wish not to be extricated or possibly even extradited back to Egypt and have to re-enter the very feared S and M Bondage House of Ordeal:* sacrifices, *especially mass human ones,* tithes, and first-fruits must be offered *on an altar* in one only place, *which hasn't yet been established: and* all eating of blood *(and drinking of flesh)* is *positively* prohibited.

Are you ignominious Israelite Idiots dense, or what? Again, these are the *essential* precepts and judgments, that you *dumb fucks* must do in the land, which the Lord, the God of thy three *senile dead* fathers, will give thee *after you blundering dunderheads successfully invade and conquer it,* to possess it all the days that thou shalt walk, *sprint, hobble, amble, scurry or crawl* upon the *vile* Earth *and next swim across and/or float upon the hungry crocodile-infested Jordan Torrent.*

Destroy all the places in which the nations, that you shall possess, *have* worshiped their *false lava-assed* gods upon high *treacherous* mountains, and upon *designated mole* hills, and under every shady tree, *where shady-character pagans tend to congregate and plot unwarranted rebellion.*

Overthrow their *sacrilegious* altars, and break-down their *molten lava* statues *while avoiding your own mental break-downs; shatter their volcanic lava lamps,* burn their *groovy* groves with fire *and flaming hot olive oil,* and *violently* break their idols *and their hypocritical priests* in pieces: destroy their names out of those *impious* places, *even if you might get shingles from touching their building's low overhanging name and trade/occupation signs.*

You shall not do so *in a similar manner* to the Lord your God *or else you'll each have to swallow ten gallons of whale sperm juice all in one big gulp.* But you shall come to the *unidentified and unknown* place, which the Lord your God shall choose out of all your *clannish* tribes, to put His name *up* there, and to dwell in it *after major widespread pagan ethnic cleansing has ultimately occurred.*

And you shall offer in that *unknown yet-to-be-identified* place your holocausts *along with your pagan holocaust victims,* the tithes and first-fruits of your hands and your vows and gifts, *but mostly your recent thefts obtained,* the firstborn of your herds and your sheep, *and also the first, second, third and fourth born of the evil pagans, who sometimes organize into wild traveling terror gangs rapidly moving from town to town.*

And you shall eat there in the sight of the Lord your God *at the unknown unidentified desert and beach last resort:* and you shall *pretentiously* rejoice in all things, whereunto you shall put your hand, *your elbow, your ass,* yourself and your houses, *and your fertile genitals* wherein the Lord your God hath *righteously* blessed you *without your former knowledge.*

You shall not do there the things we do here this day, every man that which seemeth good to himself, *having and exhibiting an excess of PRIDE, especially during reprehensible gay parades and unorthodox trans-gender mass orgies.*

For until this present time you are not come to rest, *for there is no rest for the weary, even though you lazy louts are never evidently fatigued.* And to the *ongoing* possession, *I suggest that you keep your eyes on the lucrative secret prize,* which the Lord your God will give you *after you have adequately pilfered and kept it.*

You shall pass over the Jordan *while excitedly riding upon imported fully-grown river alligators,* and shall dwell *underground* in the land which the Lord your God will give you, that you may have *subterranean* rest *and escape* from all *pagan* enemies *roaming* round about *in all the area roundabouts:* and may dwell without any fear, *because you might wind-up assassinated and dead quicker than you can recite from memorization the Greek Geek Alphabet in reverse order.*

In the *shadowy unknown yet-to-be-identified* place, which the Lord your God shall choose *from names pinned onto a carnival spinning wheel,* that His *revered* name may be therein *and imaginatively called Godville at each chance stop of the rotating wheel.* Thither shall you bring all the things that I *emphatically* command you, holocausts, *holocaust victims, pagan captives, looted plunder* and tithes, vegetable cakes, the first-fruits of your hands, *home-made fruitcakes, gay fruitcakes, fruit of the loom, and the fruit of thy ladies' wombs too:* and whatsoever is the choicest in the gifts which you shall vow to the Lord, *which you have constructively and beneficially stolen from the nearby pagans.*

There shall you feast *somewhere in the religious retreat of Godville* before the *consenting* Lord, you and your sons and your daughters, your menservants and maidservants, *your adulterous girlfriends, your wife's adulterous girlfriends, your concubines and your sex-crazed prostitutes,* and the *meandering* Levite that dwelleth in your cities, *easily recognized by virtue of their blue canvas pants and exposed denim underwear.* For He' hath no other part and possession among you *other than that which you can greedily steal from the rich, conquered-but-docile pagans.*

Beware lest thou offer thy *animal, vegetable, mineral and human* holocausts in every place that thou shalt see: But in the *geographic* place which the Lord shall choose in one of thy tribes, *namely yet to be located Godville,* shalt thou offer *immense* sacrifices, and shalt do all *activities* that I command thee, *or else you'll have to involuntarily take my lonely frustrated place as the Lord's sole soul prophet.*

But if thou desirest to eat, *drink and be merry,* and the eating of flesh *or luscious fish-smelly pussy* delight thee, kill, and eat according to the blessing of the Lord thy God, which He hath given thee, in thy *manifold defeated* cities: whether it be unclean, *or maybe too dry and hairy,* that is to say, having *venereal* blemish or defect: or *possibly merely* clean *blotches or boils,* that is to say, sound and without *major* blemish, *wet and pink and juicy too,* such as may be offered, as the roe, and the stout hart, *and the delicious pussy cat,* shalt thou eat it *raw and then lick thy lips in total satisfaction.*

Only the blood thou shalt not eat, but thou shalt pour it out upon the Earth as water *before ever ravishingly consuming the accompanying delectable red flesh.* Thou mayst not eat in thy towns the tithes of thy corn, and thy wine, and thy oil, *and thy new slave women recently obtained, and* the firstborn *of the last born,* and thy herds *of chickens* and thy *recently stolen scrawny* cattle *too,* nor any thing that thou vowest *or wish to have on whim,* and that thou wilt offer voluntarily *(if not wilted) to thy chamberlain,* and the first-fruits of thy hands *now full with itchy peach fuzz.*

But thou shalt eat them before the Lord thy God in the place which the Lord thy God shall choose, *the yet-to-be-built Godville,* thou and thy son and thy *incestual* daughter, and thy *gay faggot* manservant, and thy *accommodating* maidservant *whore,* and the *fierce* Levite *pedophile* that dwelleth in thy cities' *perverted blue jean sectors:* and thou shalt rejoice and be refreshed before the Lord thy God in all things, whereunto thou shalt put *over thy heart* thy hand, *thy stinky middle finger, and wherever thy will instinctively insert thy erect throbbing sex gland.*

Take heed thou forsake not the Levite all the time that thou livest in the *vanquished* land, *for some day heavy blue canvas pantalones will become the vogue once we Israelites learn to forever disrobe our ugly filthy robes.*

When the Lord thy God shall have enlarged thy borders, *allowing illegal aliens to become Jews* as He hath *often* spoken to thee *when you tawdry assholes are busy screwing and sucking one another in your stench-laden straw beds,* and thou wilt eat the flesh that thy soul desireth, *but first you frivolous jerk-offs must become politically correct and wholeheartedly admit the minions of lazy illegal gay aliens into Godville City Limits.*

And if the *not-on-any-map* place which the Lord thy God shall choose, *namely Godville,* that His *awesome sacred* name should appear *on a variety of building shingles* there, be far off, thou shalt kill of thy herds and of thy flocks, as I have commanded thee, and shalt eat in thy towns good and a-plenty, *as it pleaseth thee before then crazily traveling by foot across the hot arid desert to the unknown destination known as Godville, where Hebrew destination weddings with non-pagans will in the near future become an accepted Jewish tradition, along with occasional bar-mitzvahs too.*

Even as the roe and the hart are *ravenously* eaten *as if we are voracious Hebrew blackbirds,* so shalt thou eat them: *so let the sinful pagans eat crow and us being left to consume the cawing ravens alive;* both the clean and unclean shall eat of them alike, *for our chosen supper desserts are for the birds and for us human birdbrains alike to sample.*

Only beware of this *monotonous redundancy,* that thou eat not the blood *platelets* or *the thin liquid protoplasm,* for the blood is *intended* for the soul *to be nourished at a future date:* and therefore thou must not eat the soul with the flesh, *even if it is described by the inconsiderate pagan restaurant waiter as "gourmet soul food."*

But thou shalt pour it *(the rich blood and the thin protoplasm)* upon the Earth as water, that it` may be well with thee and thy *fickle epicurean* children after thee, when thou shalt do that which is pleasing in the sight of the Lord. *And if you notice that you have pissed blood one morning when urinating out the open window, whatever you do, don't drink or consume it, or else you will have committed a mortal sin-type abomination of the highest magnitude.*

But the things which thou hast sanctified and vowed to the Lord, thou shalt take *as if it was stolen property from a lowlife pagan's house,* and shalt come to the place which the Lord shall choose, *namely Godville, nestled in its rustic rural desert vicinity.* And *there in somnolent Godville* shalt offer thy oblations, the flesh and the blood upon the altar of the Lord thy God: the blood of thy *innocent* victims thou shalt *maniacally* pour onto the *now-altered rickety* altar: and the flesh thou thyself shalt eat. *We shall perform this bizarre ritual until Godville finally grows in size from a tiny bazaar into God City.*

Observe and hear all the things that I *Moses* command thee, that it may be well with thee and thy *illegitimate non-pagan* children after thee forever, when thou shalt do what is good and pleasing in the sight and *super-vision* of the Lord thy God, *but when He's traveling away on a supernatural vacation, who knows what the hell havoc you'll be doing in His brief absence!*

When the Lord thy God shall have destroyed before thy face the nations *you have aggressively conquered and plundered,* which thou shalt go in to possess *after everything there has been completely obliterated,* and when thou shalt possess them, *even the broken pottery jugs and the smashed urns formerly artistically decorated with naked lava-pissing pagan gods and goddesses embossed around their circumference,* and you *O Israel will* dwell in their land *as proud non-celibate Hebrews, an aberrant carefree race always enjoying fucking around.*

Beware lest thou imitate them, *the now roving, nomadic, very dangerous fast-moving pagan donkey cart gangs,* and after they are destroyed at thy *triumphant* coming into *Godville,* and lest thou seek after their *heathen* ceremonies, saying: "As these nations have worshiped their *charlatan* gods, so will I also worship *in Godville until the prosperous hamlet evolves and develops into Metropolitan God City.* "

Thou shalt not do in like manner to the Lord thy God*'s permanent property, which is now your temporary property that can be confiscated* from you *by me Moses any time at my sole discretion or whim.* For they *(the radical pagans)* have done to their gods all the abominations which the Lord abhorreth, offering their sons and daughters, and burning them with *intense* fire, *and wildly drinking the molten lava being shot out of the pagan god statues' erect penises and from their enormous pulsating mechanical assholes.*

What I command thee, *you thick-skulled Israelite loons, is* that only do thou to the Lord: neither add anything', nor diminish anything. *Just leave everything in your immediate environment the fuck alone; that is, if you dim-minded shit-heads know what the hell's good for you.*

That only *you should* do thou, etc... They *(the incorrigible Israelites and their lackluster descendants)* are *emphatically* forbidden here *(or anywhere in the prospective planned Godville vicinity)* to follow the *vile* ceremonies, *rituals, sacrifices, traditions and extraditions* of the *foul sex-crazed* heathens; or to make any alterations in the divine *ordinances that I am enumerating without first obtaining my expressed permission and final approbation.*

Chapter Thirteen

"The Penalties for Idolatry"

False prophets, *especially the female ones wearing falsies and breast enhancements,* must be slain, and *all the* idolatrous cities destroyed *before MGC (Metropolitan Godville City) can be officially constructed and consecrated.* If there rise in the midst of thee a *rival bogus* prophet or one that saith he hath dreamed a *revolutionary* dream, and he foretell a sign and a wonder like *a streaking naked comet or perhaps a flaming nude meteor, yelling-out to you like a deluded maniac in fucked-up lunatic fashion, "I have a dream!" then O Israel, I highly recommend that you just ignore the preposterous bastard and quickly report the arrogant shit-head to me (Moses) so that the ingrate newcomer/amateur asshole may be swiftly stoned to death or promptly executed on the spot.*

And that come to pass which he *(the itinerant pretend impostor prophet)* spoke, and he say to thee *just like any vile pagan would perpetually elucidate:* "Let us go and follow strange gods *for a change of pace, weirdo gods* which thou knowest not, and let us serve and worship them, *for instance, learning how to make rough coarse soap from cooled-off lava in the complicated educational process."* But thou shalt not hear the words of that *phony* prophet *or the illogical rhetoric of that ambitious day*dreamer: for the Lord your God trieth you *with this stiff competition to my assumed authority,* that it *(this absurd opposing religious viewpoint stuff)* may appear whether you love him *(the bullshit new prophet impersonator)* with all your *tangible* heart, and with all your *non-tangible* soul *or not, and I (Moses) must attest that the raunchy son-of-a-bitch rookie is basically at best a blustering bullshit artist vainly attempting to capitalize on my widespread notoriety! This new imaginary prevaricating prophet shall not profit from my hard labor, dedication and effort!*

Now the Almighty Lord one day said that I should stay away from Chapter Thirteen just like future Caesar should stay away from the Ides of March, but quite candidly, I don't know or care what the hell He was radically talking about. He then mentioned that I should stay away from false prophets just like "future disingenuous cooking-the-books" corporations should do, and that vague nebulous statement

75

of His also drastically confused my normal cerebral functioning. All I really know is that we Israelites ought to follow the Lord our God, and fear Him *and His vindictive mercurial temper,* and keep His Commandments, and hear His voice, *the one that only I can perceive:* Him you shall serve *with singing hymns,* and to Him you shall cleave *to as if the Ten Commandments of His were stunning women's cleavage.*

And that *fake* prophet or forger of dreams shall be slain *because this valueless place is my promised territory and this piss-poor oasis is too small for the two of us:* because he *(the non-existent false prophet)* spoke to draw you away from the Lord your God, Who *wisely* brought you out of the land of Egypt, *(well honestly now, He did it by appointing me as your fearful leader),* and *He* redeemed you from the *horrendous* house of bondage and *the gruesome torture racks situated inside the terrible S and M edifice back in beautiful Egypt, where we all needed fuckin' Cairo chiropractors to have our anatomies adjusted by cruel Egyptian crack-pots when it finally came-down to crunch time.*

If thy brother, the son of thy mother *or girlfriend,* or thy son, or daughter, or thy wife's *boyfriend's* son or daughter that is in thy bosom *when the fetus ought to be in the woman's womb,* or thy *gay trans-gender* friend, whom thou lovest as thy own *blithe perverted* soul, would persuade thee secretly, saying: "Let us go, and serve strange *lesbian* gods *with molten lava assholes weirdly behaving like active volcanoes,* which thou knowest not, nor thy fathers, *nor thy three fathers' now-deceased trans-gender friends knew either, many centuries ago. Beware, or else have your tender ass vulcanized!*

Of all the nations round about *in the area roundabouts and perplexing cul-de-sacs too,* that are near or afar off from *the stenchy public outhouses,* from one end of the *flat square* Earth to the other, *I say this indisputable truth to you dumb-fuck bipolar geography students.* Consent not to him, *the imaginary false prophet preaching consensual sex and adultery.* And hear him not; neither let thy eye spare him to pity and conceal him, *the major eyesore, for the pretend pretender is truly a pretentious asshole that needs to be vulcanized.*

But thou shalt presently put him to death, *so execute the necessary theoretical deed right away after this imaginary competitor of mine shows-up in* Godville *or its outskirts.* Let thy hand be first upon him, and afterwards the *left* hands of all the people *so that we craven Israelites can invent what will be known in the distant future as "the one-hand strangle."*

Presently put him *(the imaginary false prophet)* to death... Not by killing him by private *unlawful* authority, but by *right away* informing the *vigilante* magistrate, and proceeding by order of *the sexually abstinent* Justice *of the Piece, and if he's not around or on vacation, allow the local pedophile priest or bisexual rabid rabbi to molest and then murder the imaginary false prophet who has been absolutely plaguing my all-too-vulnerable mind.*

With stones shall he be stoned to death *until he's stone-cold dead:* because he *(the false hypothetical fantasy prophet)* would have withdrawn thee from the Lord thy God, Who *(with my indispensable help)* brought thee out of the land of Egypt, *salvaging thee* from the *dreaded S and M* House of Bondage. That all Israel hearing may fear *being slowly tortured and killed like the false imaginary prophet shall be swiftly dispensed with,* and may do no more thing like this *erroneous speech giving crap I'm now communicating, or else the lunatic pedophile local rabbi will take over the cut-and-dry beheading persecution/prosecution.* If in one of thy cities, *towns, bergs, omelets or hamlets,* which the Lord thy God shall give thee to dwell in, thou hear some *misguided itinerant assholes* say: "Children of Belial are gone out of the midst of thee, and have withdrawn the inhabitants of their city, and *waiters and waitresses in slow-food restaurants* have said: 'Let us go, and serve strange gods which you know not'."

Belial... That is, without yoke *or egg whites for breakfast.* Hence the wicked, who refuse to be subject to the *written-in-stone* Divine Law, are called in *unwritten* scripture *(written by future Biblical jerk-off scribes)* "the children of Belial."

Inquire carefully and diligently, the truth of the thing by looking well into it, *just like an amateur proctologist closely examines a regular, ordinary asshole,* and if thou find that which is said to be certain, and that this abomination hath been really committed, *immediately remove the abomination as if it were a bothersome hemorrhoid or a painful gigantic wooden splintery dildo.*

Thou shalt forthwith kill the inhabitants of that *alienated* city with the edge of the sword, and shalt destroy it and all things that are in it, even the cattle *in the herds that have not heard the Lord's truth. Those atheist cattle too must be neuterized and then pastureized.*

And all the household goods that are there, thou shalt gather together in the midst of the *filthy* streets thereof, *especially when militant garbage collectors are on strike again,* and shall burn them *(the goods; not the militant garbage collectors)* with the city itself, so as to consume all for the Lord thy God, and that it be a *rubbish* heap forever, *specifically meaning taking no more dumps in the city dump:* it *(the city and the city dump)* shall be built no more, *not even the scorched and torched fire department buildings that have been destroyed by deliberate arson.*

And there shall be nothing of that anathema stick to thy hand, *to thy chest, to thy penis, to thy testicles or to thy accursed asshole:* that the *volatile unpredictable* Lord may turn from the wrath of His fury, and may have *bountiful* mercy on thee, and multiply thee as He swore to thy *three main disillusioned* fathers, *who incidentally all screwed many, many women, both straight and lesbian whores.*

When thou shalt hear the *bellowing* voice of the Lord thy God *like I do every single morning, noon, and night,* keeping all His *arbitrary* precepts, which I command thee this day *to wholly honor and obey,* that thou mayst do what is pleasing to the sight, *ears, smell, taste and touch of the Almighty Lord thy God.*

Chapter Fourteen

"Pagan Mourning Rites"

In *morning* mourning for the dead they *(the wicked pagans)* are not to follow the ways *and means' committees* of the *gentle* Gentiles, *most of whom in my estimation are practicing pagans and heathens anyway, or maybe even combinations of both accursed entities:* the distinction of clean and unclean meats *is exceptionally clear as mud:* ordinances concerning tithes, and first-fruits *and first-fruit flies have been well-defined in my private conversations with the Lord. And I advise that you husbands solely use your pork to screw your wife, who may not eat your pork, but only occasionally suck on it when she is menstruating.*

Be ye children of the Lord your Almighty God: you shall not cut yourselves, nor make any baldness for the dead; *and if a bald person dies, have a hairy idea and impetuously cut-off your hair and glue it to the corpse's head before he or she is officially buried.*

Because thou' art a *wholly* holy people to the Lord thy God: and He *scrupulously* chose thee alone to be His peculiar people of all *peculiar* nations that are *nomadically wandering around* upon the *peculiar* Earth. Eat not the things that are unclean, *especially dirty smelly pussy and definitely gross-smelling un-wiped butt-holes.*

These are the beasts that you shall eat: the ox, and the sheep, and the goat *with or without goatees,* the hart and the roe, *the Nile crocodile, the ape-shit gorilla,* the wild goat *without the goatee, the Yogi bear, the weasel* and the *spotless leopard.*

Every beast that divideth the hoof in two parts, and cheweth the cud, you shall eat *to thy' heart's and to thy stomach's content.* But of them that chew the *cuddly* cud, but divide not the hoof, you shall not eat, such as the camel, *the wildebeest, either gnu or old,* the hare, and *the Molasses Tortoise from Manasses:* because they chew the cud, *and not the fat as we Hebrews do,* but divide not the hoof *like heifers do;* they *(the divided hoofers)* shall be *regarded as* unclean to you.

The swine also *should be understood,* because it divideth the hoof, but cheweth not the cud, shall be unclean; their flesh you shall not *pig-out on* or *avariciously* eat *in the rock stadium refreshment area,* and their carcasses you shall not touch. *And when driving your primitive obsolete donkey cart on the open dirt trail, don't be pig-headed and hog the damned road in an unclean boarish manner, meaning "Don't litter!"* And in addition, tell your domestic cats and dogs not to litter also, so that we can have adequate animal population control in Godville and vicinity without every female animal feeling a need to literally litter.*

These shall you eat of all that abide in the *fresh* waters, *in the fish-tanks and in dirty unkempt home aquariums:* All that have fins and scales, you shall eat *after weighing yourselves on the aforementioned scales.* Such *sea creatures that* are without fins and scales, you shall not eat, because they are unclean, *unless you clean the shrimp, clams, oysters, crabs and lobsters yourself. Many jubilant blind Hebrews actually benefit from this sort of unclean sea-food diet.*

All birds that are clean you shall eat, *my fine feathered friends.* The unclean *having full bowels* eat not: to wit, the eagle, and the *grieving griping* grype, and the *oprah* osprey *and the night owl, who doesn't give a hoot whether it is eaten or not. But confidentially, your unfaithful wife or girlfriend may eat the bird, or you may munch on her nest when she's not bleeding periodically.*

The ringtail hawk, *the flying ringtail raccoon,* and the *scavenging* vulture, and the *flying* kite *along with the screaming children flying kites,* all according to their *individual* kind: And all of the raven's kind *as far away as the River Po:* And the *almost-extinct ostracized* ostrich, and the *Lazarus* Larus *that always looks dead,* and the *market merchandise peddling* hawks, according to its kind.

The heron, *and the heroine goosing goose' not on heroin,* and the *swooning* swan, and the *stark* stork' *when not busy delivery screaming babies.* And the *all-too-abundant* cormorant', the *common* porphirion, and *also* the rebellious night *gym* crow *too. And let's not forget* the *biting* bittern, and the *overpopulated* charadrion, everyone in their *fucked-up* kind: the *hula* houp also and the *embattled battalion* bat.

Everything that creepeth and *gives us the creeps,* and hath little wings *that are tasty when deep-fried,* shall be unclean, and shall not be eaten. But whatsoever is *already* dead of itself, eat not thereof, *or else instantly become decaying road-kill yourself.* Give it *(the nauseous road-kill)* to the *old buzzard* stranger *so that he can die and be gobbled-up by voracious condors and turkey vultures,* that is within thy gates *and your walking gaits,* to eat, or sell it to him, *the anonymous targeted stranger who might just be the imaginary prophet impersonator in alien disguise:* because thou art the *wholly* holy people of the Lord thy God, *who absolutely love absurd redundancy as much as I do.* And then too, thou shalt not boil a kid in the milk of his dam, *not even one of your own obnoxious kids. But whatever you do, don't carry-on with the already dead carrion!*

Every year thou shalt set aside the tithes of all thy fruits, *vegetables, worms, rats, ants and other revolting insects* that the Earth bringeth forth. And thou shalt eat before the Lord thy God in the place which He shall choose, *stealthily referred to as top-secret Godville,* that His *soon-to-be-patented* name may be called upon therein, the tithe of thy corn, *thy corns, thy bunions, thy planters' warts, thy heel calluses, thy hammer-head toes,* and thy wine, and thy *cholesterol* oil, and the firstborn of thy herds and thy sheep *always escaping on the lam:* that thou mayst learn to fear the Lord thy God at all times. *Live in fear or else die, O Israel! That is the Almighty Lord's 3 M's; mantra, maxim and motto!*

But when the way and the place which the Lord thy God shall choose, are far off, *let's say that Godville is in Siberia for example,* and He hath blessed thee *for no special reason at all,* and thou canst not carry all these things thither *all the way north to the frozen Arctic.* Thou shalt sell them all, and turn your *traded* property into money, and shalt carry it in thy *cumbersome* hand, and shalt go to the place which the Lord shall choose *and there you must then build magnificent igloos and ice castles to simulate the frigid weather conditions prevalent in Siberia, where the horniest women are also frigid.*

And thou shalt buy with the same money *(wooden coins)* whatsoever pleaseth thee, either of the herds or of sheep, *or perhaps torn condoms, unsanitary napkins or iron trusses,* or *sour* wine also and strong drink *like Siberian vodka too,* and all that thy *starving* soul desireth: and thou shalt eat *good-and-plenty without any*

81

contemptible snickers evident upon your faces before the Lord thy God, and thou shalt feast, thou and thy *hungry* house *that thou live in, in thou community, in thou nation, in thou section of thou pleasant Metropolitan Godville City.*

And the Levite that is within thy gates, beware thou forsake him not, because he hath no other part in thy possession *except his denim blue jeans, right now his only skin in the game. Teach him farming and agriculture so that he can have a farm like Old McMoses, and then the Levite can easily fill 'the gap' between rich and poor and eventually, he'll have enough money to start a viable Godville garment district.*

The third year thou shalt separate another tithe of all things that grow to thee at that time, and shalt lay it up within thy gates, *but nowhere near the Lord's Pearly Gates, which are presently forbidden and off-limits to dead former mortals. I mean, as long as Heaven is closed to mortal souls, who gives a shit whether it's there or not? What's in it for us restricted Jews?*

And the Levite that hath no other part *in God's dramatic tragic stage play* nor possession with thee, and the *non-pagan* stranger, and the fatherless *illegitimates* and the *sex-starved window* widow, that are *cavorting around* within thy *rusty squeaky front* gates, shall come and shall eat and be filled *and fulfilled too:* that the Lord thy God may bless thee in all the works *and fireworks* of thy *untrustworthy* hands that thou shalt do *when not contemplating suicide and considering final escape from our shared totally bullshit reality.*

Chapter Fifteen

"Debts and the Poor"

The law of the seventh year is of remission, *although few of us Hebrews are afflicted with terminal cancer.* The firstlings of cattle are to be sanctified to the Lord, *and when this process happens, we must all chant in unison, "Holy cow!"* In the seventh year thou shalt make a remission b*y giving your cow cancer and then attempting to cure it by igniting and smoking a camel in the smokehouse.*

Which *day* shall be celebrated in this' *illogical chronological* order? He to whom anything is owed from his friend or neighbor or brother, cannot demand it again, because it is the year of remission of the Lord. *So in regard to your neighbor' who owes you scads of money, try giving him cancer so that his accumulative debts can be satisfactorily remitted during remission.*

Of the foreigner or stranger thou mayst exact *or extort* it: of thy countryman and neighbor thou shalt not have power to demand it again, but *by all means* price-gouge the *distrustful son-of-a-bitch* foreigner, *the stranger, the alien, the pagan and the heathen, and do it in a similar manner as to how yesterday you had cleverly price-gouged your naïve Hebrew neighbor.*

And although the Lord despises socialism, there shall be neither poor nor beggars among you: that the Lord thy God may bless thee in the land which He will give thee in possession, *and once Levi establishes the proposed Godville Garment Manufacturing District, capitalism will be born and employment prosperity will flourish all throughout our burgeoning theocracy. But first Levi must secure permission for the admirable project from the Lord's Celestial Zoning Board Commission.*

There shall be no poor, *but only destitute prostitutes in Godville Proper.* This is not to be understood as a *promiscuous* promise, that there should be no poor *welfare recipients* in Israel *since no costly welfare system will ever be established.* We have learned that God's people would never be at a loss to find objects for their charity, *slickly stealing items from enemy drawers, from pagan boxer shorts' drawers and from worn and ragged heathen dirty grimy underwear, from wallets and purses, and from various items furtively purloined from thy neighbor's desks and bedroom bureaus.* But it is an ordinance that all should do their best endeavors to prevent any of their *impoverished* brethren from suffering the *adversities and* hardships of *community* poverty and want, *and if everybody steals from everyone else, we'll have the perfect economy with no rich assholes to ever complain about and envy.*

Yet so if thou hear the Voice of the Lord thy God, *you might in truth be delusional just like I fuckin' am, but just to be on the safe side,* keep all things that He hath ordained, *except the rabbis and the priests who have not yet been officially ordained,* and *keep the instructions* which I command thee this day; He will bless thee, as He hath *incessantly* promised *over and over again.*

Thou shalt *enthusiastically* lend to many nations *at exorbitant loan-shark interest rates,* and thou shalt borrow of no man, *especially those devious con-artist strangers that try to always Jew you down.* Thou shalt have dominion over very many nations, *of which I can't currently name any,* and no one shall have *unscrupulous* dominion over thee, *except the Almighty Lord and me.*

If one of thy brethren that dwelleth within thy gates of thy city in the land which the Lord thy God will give thee, *namely Godville, but then later hopefully evolving into God City,* come to poverty: thou shalt not harden thy heart, nor close thy hand to a brother Hebrew, *but alluding to the pestilence of annoying gentiles and pagans, well then jubilant Jew, that's another friggin' story.*

But shalt open it *(your house and finances)* to the poor man, thou shalt lend him, that which thou perceivest he hath need of *and not what the poor bastard actually asks you for.* Beware lest perhaps a wicked thought steal in upon thee *and it makes you think for the first time in your piss-poor life,* and thou say in thy *tongue-less* heart: "The seventh year of remission draweth nigh"; and thou turn away thy eyes from thy poor *seven-year-old* brother, denying to lend him that which he asketh: *no allowance from you for the neighbor's little prick kid either,* lest he cry against thee to the Lord, and it then becomes a sin unto thee *that you then buy the little brat large square wooden marbles so that the destructive miniature monster could*

84

throw the solid objects at your stone house and happily break your windows and your balls too.

But thou shalt *generously* give to him, *the repulsive punk kid next door:* neither shalt thou do anything craftily in relieving his necessities, *like making him drink a good amount of prune juice to ease his chronic constipation*: that the Lord thy God may bless thee at all times, and in all things to which thou shalt put thy hand, *including around the punk kid's despicable throat.*

There will not be wanting poor in the land of thy habitation. *Who the hell wants poor people, beggars, mendicants, hobos, tramps and pan-handlers living next door?* Therefore I *(Moses)* command thee, *from my lonely command center here in not yet established Godville,* to open thy *non-amputated* hand to thy needy and poor brother, that liveth in the land, *before one onerous jerk-off resorts to felony crime and the villain unexpectedly robs your ass blind. Even if you are a reputable optometrist, the detestable punk will still rob you blind!*

When thy brother, a *peculiar* Hebrew man, *or active Hebrew woman transvestite, or perhaps a Hebrew man/woman trans-sexual* is sold to thee, and hath served thee six years, in the seventh year thou shalt let him/her go free *and further pervert the liberal receptive society that's out there.* And when thou sendest him out *into the real world free,* thou shalt not let him go away empty: *provide him with a box of condoms and with another box of handy ass wipes too.*

But shall give him for his way out *one* of thy flocks, and out of thy barn floor, and thy winepress, wherewith the Lord thy God shall bless thee *for not allowing your former trans-gender servant to pull the cotton-picking wool over your gullible eyes, for not allowing him to intentionally leave the barn door open, and finally, for not permitting him or her to squeeze and crush your delicate testicles in the family winepress, for the Lord despises all vice, including the one inside the fuckin' winepress.*

Remember that thou also wast a *past* bondservant in the land of Egypt, *where you were perpetually raped and sodomized daily,* and the Lord thy God made thee free, and therefore I now command thee *this declaration of religious dependence.* But if he *(the sexually confused manservant)* says *stupid bullshit like this:* "I will not depart: because I loveth thee, and thy house," and *the presumptuous asshole* findeth that he is well with thee: *then swiftly kick the parasitic moocher's ass right out the front door, for he or she surely deserved a good swift kick in the ass a long time coming.*

Thou shalt take an *awful* awl, and bore through his ear in the door of thy house, *going and drilling from the lobe to perform a vital lobotomy,* and he shall *then* serve thee forever: thou shalt do in like manner to thy woman-servant also, *but in her unique case, forget the ear and drill her hot wet vagina really good, again and again.*

Turn not away thy eyes from them when thou makest them free, *or else he or she (the departing servant) might amply steal from you, or better yet, might amply kill you, and then by sheer luck you'll accidentally achieve freedom from the Vengeful Lord's stringent Commandments.* Because he *(the trans-gender manservant)* hath served thee six years according to the laws *and according to the National Sex Employee Wage Charts* of a hireling: that the Lord thy God may bless thee in all the works that thou dost *in order for thee to be respectably buried in the village dust dump, without any hope of ever achieving Heaven, which is now exclusively limited to the Lord and his big-shot bodyguard archangels.*

Of the firstlings', that come of thy herds and thy sheep *and thy rambunctious rams,* thou shalt sanctify to the Lord thy God whatsoever is of the male sex, *but in the case of bisexual trans-gender sheep, it is hard and confusing to tell the difference in male as opposed to female genitalia.* Thou shalt not work with the firstling of a bullock, and thou shalt not shear the firstlings of thy sheep *simply for the sake of sheer shearing pleasure.*

In the sight of the Lord thy God shalt thou eat them *(the non-zoo animal parts)* every year, in the *bustling village tavern, in the boisterous village beer garden, or* in the place that the Lord shall choose, thou and thy house, *or perhaps in Godville, once the fantasy metropolis is eventually planned and fully constructed.*

But if it *(the gift animal)* have a blemish, or be lame, or blind, or in any part disfigured or feeble, it shall not be sacrificed to the Lord thy God, but instead, eaten by the *fucked-up trans-gender* servants *still in your employ. Frankly, those sinning bastards and bitches would eat anything, including cocks, beavers, minks, foxy foxes, pussies and any Tom (turkey), Dickey and harried Harry.*

But thou shalt eat it *(the already itemized domesticated animals)* within the gates of thy *future* city, *so make sure not to get your dense dunce heads caught between the narrow vertical iron bars:* the clean and the unclean shall eat them alike, as the roe and as the hart, *that is, eat them whole where the deer and the antelope do not roam.*

Only thou *fellow Hebrew* shalt take heed not to eat their blood *or drink their flesh,* but instead pour it out onto the Earth as water, *otherwise you might be reincarnated upon the Earth, wondrously reappearing as one of the deformed animals you had just consumed at the convenient village tavern or neighborhood beer garden. I mean, who the hell wants to live again, even as a lowly animal?*

Chapter Sixteen

"Feast of the Passover"

The three principal solemnities to be observed *and implemented are generally as follows:* just judges *(according to the inflexible Divine Laws)* to be appointed in every city: all occasions of idolatry to be avoided *and punishable by excruciating death in the public square or in the rock stadium arena.* Observe the month of new corn, which is the first of the spring *when both square dances and corny humor are temporarily legal,* that thou mayst celebrate the phase to the Lord thy God: because in this month the *unfazed* Lord thy God brought thee out of Egypt by night *and He wants us to be on guard against savage stalkers, particularly pagan and heathen corn field stalkers and other suspicious molesters spying on us Israelites from atop distant obelisks.*

And thou shalt sacrifice the kernels and the *pagan Colonels and Generals* in Phase One to the *unfazed* Lord thy God, of sheep, and of oxen, *and of pedigree horses and of thoroughbred dogs* in the place which the Lord thy God shall choose, *to be situated somewhere in metropolitan downtown Godville,* that His *glorious* name may dwell there *on every single building shingle and engraved brick.*

Thou shalt not eat with it *(the aforementioned kernels, Colonels and Pagan Generals)* leavened bread: seven days shalt thou eat without leaven *or leavin',* the *moldy* bread of affliction, because thou camest out of Egypt in fear *of castration, amputation, decapitation and mass mutilation:* that thou mayst remember the day of thy *gayily* coming out of *the* Egypt *closet, of Moses and the Lord parting the Red Sea without a magical comb, and last but not least,* all the days of thy *accursed immigrant* life *here while residing in Canaan.*

No leaven shall be seen in all thy coasts for seven days *until the coast is clear,* neither shall any of the flesh of that which was sacrificed the first day in the evening remain until morning, *so now we exploited and bewildered Israelites ought to eat everything with meat or red blood on the table, or else risk becoming consumable meat and red blood ourselves.*

Thou mayst not immolate the phase in any one of thy *non-existent* cities, which the Lord thy God will give thee, *but then had ordered us to enthusiastically destroy and plunder because the cities were vile, once belonging to pagans, heathens, gentiles and rich Jewish aristocrats who had made huge fortunes in the Egyptian stock and bond market, which sold shackles and chains specifically to be worn by Israelites lazily slaving in captivity.*

But in the place which the Lord thy God shall choose, *(as a hint it starts with a G and ends with an E),* that His *supreme* name may dwell there *on the marquee above some prominent contemporary Palace entertainer named Diana Rosetta Stone:* thou shalt immolate the phase in the evening, at the going down of the sun, at which time thou camest out of Egypt, *and all girls named Dawn suddenly became inspired to change their first names to Dusk.*

And thou shalt dress, and eat it *(the sumptuous festival food)* in the *mystery secret* place which the Lord thy God shall choose *from a recently acquired lottery selection basket,* and in the morning rising-up thou shalt go into thy dwellings *and continue to do nothing else but dwell.*

Six days shalt thou eat *dry moldy* unleavened bread: and on the seventh day, because it is the assembly of the Lord thy God, thou shalt do no work, *just like the rest of the week, and engage in no burping, belching, pissing or shitting until after midnight on Monday morning.*

Thou shalt *calendar* number unto thee seven weeks from that day, wherein thou *was rushin' to* put the sickle to the corn *and the hammer to the hazardous petulant pagans.* And thou shalt celebrate the *raucous* festival of weeks to the Lord thy God, a voluntary oblation of thy *arthritic* hand, which thou shalt offer according to the blessing of the Lord thy God, *praying like a penitent suppliant for the joint discovery of MSM Chondroitin and Glucosamine.*

And thou shalt feast before the Lord thy God, thou, and thy son, and thy daughter, *and thy daughter's daughter-in-law,* and thy *homosexual bisexual manservant,* and thy maidservant *transvestite trans-gender personage,* and the *ostracized shunned* Levite that is within thy gates, *his large thick head still stuck between the narrow vertical iron bars.* And *also* the stranger and the fatherless, and the *black* widow *visiting from Africa,* who abide with you *and all sinfully sleep with you, all together in your small stinky straw bed:* all this *stuff will in the remote future occur* in the place which the Lord thy God shall choose *from the unlucky lotto random selection basket,* that His name may dwell there, *yes, it will dwell prominently all over Godville.*

And thou shalt remember that thou *too* wast *once* a *meager sex* servant in Egypt: and thou shalt keep and do the things that are commanded, even if they are *currently classified as* forbidden acts *like fellatio and sodomy, both atrocious abominations athletically and acrobatically performed at the same damned time.*

Thou shalt celebrate the solemnity also of tabernacles seven days, when thou hast gathered in thy fruit of the barn floor and of the winepress. *Then you must burn-down thy termite-infested barn and replace it with a common tent, for that is what a tabernacle is, a mere tent made from Levi's finest blue canvas material.*

And thou shalt make merry in thy festival time, thou, thy son, and thy daughter, *thy daughter's daughter-in-law, your other in-laws, your family outlaws,* thy *homo'* manservant, and thy *trans-gender* maidservant, the *leprous* Levite *tailor* also, and the *ominous heathen* stranger, and the fatherless *impotent rabbi* and the *fertile black* widow *spider-lady visiting your abode from Africa,* that are within thy *home's* gates *with their big heads stuck between the narrow vertical bars, but who all sleep in your small bed with you and your three excessively corpulent spouses.*

Seven days shalt thou celebrate *designated* feasts to the Lord thy God in the *secret* place which the Lord shall choose, *ostensibly predetermined as Godville:* and the Lord thy God will bless thee in all thy fruits *and in all thy gay fruitcake faggot servants too,* and in every work of thy hands *including all of your frantic climaxing hand-jobs,* and thou shalt be *exploding* in joy *during the culminating climax of the religious festival.*

Three times in a year shall all thy males appear *like magic* before the Lord thy God in the *clandestine* place which He shall choose *after the all-important basket selection lottery has commenced:* in the feast of unleavened bread, in the feast of weeks, and in the feast of tabernacles, *where everyone in the end of the wild harvest celebrations (for we are a simple and primitive agrarian culture) will feast their eyes on dancing naked nymphs and upon lying-down open-beaver nude harlots.* No one shall appear with his hands empty before the Lord, *because as has often been said, it is common knowledge that a hard bird in the hand is worth none nestled inside the dancing open-beaver and lying-down nude bushes.*

But every one shall offer *sperms and eggs* according to what he *or she* hath *to render,* according to the blessing of the Lord thy God, which He shall give him *and her before either verbal or sexual intercourse transpires later-on that special evening. And don't forget, excellent ejaculations can occur and are allowed when either speaking or screwing.*

Thou shalt appoint *pin-headed* judges and magistrates in all thy *swinging* gates *especially designed for swingers,* which the Lord thy God shall give thee to *promote the forthcoming Jewish population explosion,* in all thy *weasel-minded* tribes: that they may *subjectively* judge the people with just judgment *about their individual sexual performance, either straight or perverted.*

And not go aside to either part *of the crowded master chamber bed.* Thou shalt not accept person or gifts *to nonchalantly trade for casual or serious sex:* for gifts *tend to* blind the eyes of the wise, *suddenly making the erudite fools unwise,* and change the words of the just *from "Let's have academic verbal intercourse!" to "Hello there Stranger! Let's get wildly laid right now!"*

Thou shalt follow justly after that which is just: that thou mayst live and possess the *Promised* Land, which the Lord thy God shall give thee *to only have sexual orgies during the three already specified ceremonial events: The Annual Autumn Corn Huskers Extravaganza; The Levite Leaven Bread Bake-off, and The Nude Feast of the Dancing Tabernacles, starring that mentally unstable infidel group, Omar the Tentmaker and his Jolly Jihadists.*

Thou shalt plant no *groovy* grove, *neither orange nor olive,* nor any tree near the *rickety wooden decaying* altar of the Lord thy God: Neither shalt thou make nor set-up to thyself a statue *of Abraham,*

Martin and John all sitting together playing cards in a secluded orange or placid olive grove: which things the *very jealous and possessive* Lord thy God hateth *with a passion, since He once got into a fierce argument with the Greek Deity Zeus for maliciously attempting to steal His thunder.*

Chapter Seventeen

"Judges"

Victims must be without blemish, *jock itch or noticeable athlete's foot fungus infection.* Idolaters are to be slain *expeditiously in the public square, standing erect either in a circle or in a triangle formation. Bothersome* controversies are to be decided by the high priest and council, *sitting and consulting in the fragile stone synagogue choir loft,* whose sentence *(usually an Imperative one as opposed to a Declarative statement)* must be obeyed under pain of death, *to be administered to the entire Hebrew community.*

The duty of a king, *or if one is not readily available, the duty of a jack of all trades and a master of none,* who is to receive the law of God at the priest's *shaking palsied* hands, *that is, after an alphabet is invented and after written language finally becomes an accepted learned habit. How this improvement will happen without any schools or day care centers in functional existence still remains to be seen!*

Thou shalt not sacrifice to the Lord thy God a sheep, *an ax,* or an ox, wherein there is blemish, *or blotch, or dander, or any trace of troublesome dandruff flakes, or itchy psoriasis,* or any fault *or seismic crevice evident:* for that *irritating skin defect* is an *irritating* abomination to the Lord thy God.

When there shall be found among you within any of thy *rusty swinging swinger necking make-out gates,* which the Lord thy God shall give thee *solely for experimental romantic purposes, either* man or woman that do evil in the sight of the Lord thy God *and in public outhouses too,* and who *deliberately or unintentionally* transgress His *sacred* covenant, *then that arrogant numbskull shall be instantly executed by penetrating rectal lightning bolts before ever achieving pleasurable orgasm.*

So as to go and serve strange *pagan* gods, *whose statues possess the extraordinary lava shooting assholes,* and adore them *and their putrid-smelling lava shit,* the sun*shine and the delicious* moon*shine too,* and all the *party* hosts of Heaven, which I have not commanded *because I (Moses), like all other doomed accursed mortal beings, am* *strictly forbidden from ever entering the Lord's Exclusive Paradise Stratosphere Resort.*

The host of Heaven... That is, the *luminous* stars, *because most of us Jewish dimwits don't yet know shit about astronomical solar systems, orbiting planets, the asteroid and hemorrhoid belts, gigantic galaxies, general evolution and the existence and magnitude of the entire colossal Universe.*

And this *truth I am describing herein* is told thee, and hearing it thou hast inquired diligently, and found it to be true *knowledge originating from the verification of the several sagacious local pagan astrologers,* and that the *grievous* abomination *of selfishly seeking horoscope and zodiac readings is evilly committed* in Israel *all the fuckin' time.*

Thou shalt bring forth the man or the woman, who has committed that most wicked thing *of making love out of wedlock,* to the gates of thy city, and they shall be stoned *right after the rest of us more God-fearing inhabitants and witnesses get stoned drunk first. He who is with sin may cast the first boulder!*

By the *cannibalistic* mouths of two or three witnesses shall he' *(the accused)* die, that is to be slain *without an unnecessary trial or an unnecessary, expensive, garrulous, lying defense attorney.* Let no man be put to death, *when only one Hebrew beareth witness against him because it's then one person's word against another, but if two lying Hebrew bastards subjectively testify falsely against the third party before either a licensed priest or an incompetent theocratic judge, then that guilty son-of-a-bitch sinner must be immediately slain for the benefit of the surviving community.*

The hands of the *innocent* witnesses shall be first upon him *(the alleged perpetrator)* to kill him, and afterwards the hands of the rest of the people *seeking something to do to avoid boredom:* that thou mayst take away the evil out of the midst of thee *to make an example execution/demonstration out of the accused criminal. This proven and effective punishment method is the only way that a participating Jew can get away with bloody murder! So sayeth the Wholly Book of Doo-Doo-Rot-on-Me!*

If thou perceive that there be among you a hard and doubtful matter in judgment between blood and blood, *commonly called a family dispute or a lover's incestual quarrel, sometimes between* cause and cause, *or between* leprosy and leprosy: and thou see that the words of the *intoxicated* judges within thy gates do vary *and conflict: then* arise, and go up to the place, which the Lord thy God shall choose *but hasn't done so yet (since Godville is only in the initial planning stage). Go up front and challenge the erratic verdict and risk being fuckin' slain yourself!*

If thou perceive, etc... Here we see what authority God was pleased to give to the *aged senile* church guides *who are characteristic* of the Old Testament, in deciding life or death matters *without the aid of a qualified educated jury,* without appeal, all *simplistic* controversies relating to the law; *the forgetful, doddering, tottering senior citizens* promising that they should not err therein; and *surely* He has not done less for the *infallible* church guides of the New Testament, *which historically won't begin until a thousand years hence, so why the hell is all this cited extraneous bullshit relevant to anything?*

And thou shalt come to the *blue canvas-garbed* priests of the Levitical race, and to the *doddering geriatric* judge, that shall be at that time: *and quivering thus,* thou shalt ask of them, and they shall show thee the truth of the judgment, *because as all good Old Testament Jews fully know, it is especially easy for anyone to show a complicated abstraction in a relatively simple concrete manner.*

And thou shalt do whatsoever they *(the vigilante stoners and lynchers)* shall say, that preside in the *still-to-be-determined* place, which the Lord shall *arbitrarily* choose *in the future at His inimitable discretion,* and what they shall teach thee will *definitely* change your life *if it is you who will be unpleasantly sentenced to a painful death. Above everything else, mob rule (and its fear therein) will govern the entire land and its implementation will keep potential violators fully in check, all this community chaos enacted out of extreme fear among the ornery resident pests that they themselves might be instantaneously exterminated.*

According to His *irrefutable* law; and thou shalt follow *and complete* their 'sentence', *vaguely spoken in paragraph form*: neither shalt thou decline to the right hand nor to the left hand, *but thou shall cast stones with both available appendages, at public trials but not at raucous Jewish rock concerts.*

But he that will be proud, and refuse to obey the commandment of the *doddering senile* priest, who ministereth at that time to the Lord thy God, and the decree of the *decrepit diaper-wearing* judge, that *quickly convicted* man shall *quickly* die, and thou shalt take away the evil from Israel *by naturally committing additional evil in the Lord's Name.*

And all the people hearing and seeing it *(the unfair impromptu trial)* shall *soon* fear *a similar fate, the result afterwards suggesting* that no one *will ever* swell with pride, *which obviously is not too swell at all in terms of drastic consequences being administered to the unfortunate initial violator.*

When thou art come into the *confiscated* land, which the Lord thy God will give *benevolently* thee, and possessed it, and shalt say: "I will set a king over me, as all nations have that are round about, *including the manifold local roundabouts and the nearby dead-end cul-de-sacs too.*"

Thou shalt set him *up as king* whom the Lord thy God shall choose out of the number of thy *still-breathing* brethren. Thou mayst not make a man of another nation king, that is not thy *Jew* brother, *and bitchy queens, and Jewish princesses, and horny duchesses too, are absolutely royally forbidden in the New World Order being hereby established!*

And when he is made king, *without even playing a game of checkers,* he shall not multiply horses to himself, *for good-breeding for him is out of the question;* nor *is the new king* to lead back the *hordes of dumb-shit* people into Egypt, being lifted-up with the number of his horsemen, especially since the Lord hath commanded you to return no more the same way *to Egypt, where intelligent foreign priests and kings had severely tortured you in the dreaded S and M Nile House of Bondage, which is indeed a much less primitive practice than malevolently stoning people to death without a fair trial by jury.*

He shall not have many *cheating* wives, that may allure his mind, *for cheating wives shall be stoned in bed with their cheating adulterous male companions;* nor shall he *accumulate and* have *evil and immense* sums of silver and gold, *for money is not the root of all evil; greed is; especially intense greed for silver and gold.*

But after he *(the anonymous city mayor)* is raised to the throne of his kingdom, he shall copy-out to himself the Deuteronomy of this law in a volume, *which should take the chosen dolt only five or six years to do while we're still assiduously inventing a viable Hebrew alphabet, the newly selected king* taking the copy of the priests of the *illiterate* Levitical tribe *to duplicate for himself to study and to eventually master and then publicly declare, "I will not let this Doo-Doo-Rot-on-Me rot in me!"*

And he shall have it *(the majestic Doo-Doo-Rot-on-Me)* with him, and shall read it *(this fantastically unbelievable bullshit)* all the days of his *lackluster* life, that he may learn to fear the Lord his God, *which is what this oddball ethnocentric religion is all about besides the illegal possession of fucked-up land and property,* and keep His *indecipherable* words and *peculiar* ceremonies, that are commanded in *and throughout* the *whole suspect and capricious* law.

And without the material assistance of licensed cardiologists and certified anesthesiologists, that his *(the new king's)* heart be not lifted-up with pride over his *lowlife breathing* brethren, nor decline to the right or to the left *in terms of argumentative politics,* that he and his sons may reign *without suffering too many aneurysms* a long time over Israel, *but not over Israel in the clouds up in Heaven, which is the Almighty Lord's (and His formidable archangels') privileged domain.*

Chapter Eighteen

"Priests"

How I (humble, modest Moses) am inspired to organize this incredible bullshit text is really and truly beyond my finite mortal comprehension. How a facetious bumpkin asshole like myself' has been chosen to lead the totally nauseating Israelite jerk-offs and pussy-rubbers to randomly invade and confiscate Promised Lands is also completely unfathomable to my very limited cerebral acumen! But nevertheless, I am deeply honored to represent this immensely insane mass indoctrination!

The Lord is the inheritance of the *pedophile* priests and *the belligerent cretin* Levites, *since He is God and they are meager expendable human flesh assholes, mere pawns on His mammoth game-board.* Heathenish abominations are to be avoided *like giant falling meteors descending upon you and your doomed household. And yes,* the great PROPHET CHRIST is promised *in this rather mundane Chapter Eighteen, which in speculation might be even worse than dreaded Chapter Eleven.* False prophets must be slain *is my new central theme, hopefully as early as the aspiring upstart is occupying a manger-type cradle while un-imaginatively wrapped in swaddling clothes similar to burlap.*

The priests and Levites, and all *volatile bullies* that are of the same *atrocious unstable barbaric* tribe, shall have no part nor inheritance with the rest of *rewarded* Israel, because they shall eat the sacrifices of the Lord *as opposed to consuming ordinary table food,* and His *obligated* oblations, *all except the occasional secret tasty human sacrifices, which now are regarded as truly forbidden abominable abominations, even in distant Egypt and Mesopotamia, must be quantified, qualified and adequately defined here.*

And they *(the deliberately deprived, depraved and shunned Levites)* shall receive nothing else of the possession of their *breathing or non-breathing* brethren: for the Lord Himself is their *sole* inheritance, as He hath *often* said to them, *even to the deaf Levite tribesmen who can't hear shit but who can still perceptively see it: "Get with the program! I command that you neglected dreg*

101

*denim-makers eat the damned bloody animal sacrifices that will be
roasted and offered to Me.*"

This shall be the priest's due *diligence* from the people, and from
them that offer *sacrificial* victims *falsely accused:* whether they
sacrifice *an elephant,* an ox, *an ax* or a *prime condition* sheep, *or an
already dead previously accused human,* they shall give, *in a
mandatory fashion,* to the *doddering senile palsy-handed* priest, the
shoulder and the breast.

The first-fruits also will be taken of corn, of wine, and of palm
and skin oil, and a part of the wool from the shearing of their
sheepish sheep *offering. The coveted secrets of wine, of course, in
the future being circulating all throughout the known civilized and
uncivilized world by the wholly infamous, future Alexander the
Grape, should remain secret and coveted, for the Lord positively
loves secrets and surprises bestowed upon mankind!*

For the Lord thy God hath chosen him *(the prospective priest and
not the future conqueror Alexander the Grape)* of all thy tribes, to
stand and to minister to the name of the Lord, him and his sons
forever, *but to be only future priests and rabbis and not future
monsignors, bishops, deacons, beacons, archbishops, cardinals,
popes, conquerors or towel-headed imams.*

If a *deviate-minded* Levite goes out of any one of the cities
throughout all Israel, *which have yet to be planned or constructed,
Godville and possibly God City among them,* in which he dwelleth,
and have a longing mind *with a short memory* to *flip-a-coin and
incidentally* come to the place which the Lord shall choose, *naturally
his fine destination will have to be the back-to-the-drawing board
Godville City Limits.*

He shall minister in the name of the Lord his *Almighty* God, as
all his *breathing (inspirational)* brethren the *hostile* Levites do, that
shall stand at that time before the Lord *like mindless statues seeking
initial instructions and general guidance from deranged counselors
of the Lord, the said counselors sitting all alone and drinking coffee
and eating blood-flavored bagels down in the temple's basement
guidance office.*

He *(the unworthy suppliant Levite priest who is now worthy)* shall receive the same portion of food that the rest do: *everyone involved sharing the same tiny amount.* Besides that which is due to him' in his own *Levite* city *yet to be constructed,* by succession from his *three smart-ass dead* fathers, *who as a matter of fact didn't know shit about pronoun and noun antecedents, and silly-assed redundancies, or any more than I (Moses) do right now.*

When thou art come into the *stolen* land which the *munificent* Lord thy God shall give thee *amazingly free of charge,* beware lest thou have a mind to imitate the abominations of those *over-haughty vanquished* nations, *certain evil stuff that might immorally arouse your sinful curiosity, that might develop your mind, or that might arouse your latent libido and thus, giving you a fantastic evil erection of almost god-like proportions.*

Neither let there be found among you *dip-shit assholes* any one that shall expiate his son or daughter, making them to pass through the fire *'as-best-os' they can:* or that consulteth *charlatan* soothsayers, *who repetitiously 'say' only 'sooth' and similar dumb-shit synonyms like that,* or *who inaccurately* observeth dreams and omens *that the loony Levite mental cases crazily imagine in their deepest sleep,* neither let there be any *false* wizard *or sorcerer's apprentice practicing or preaching anywhere in God-forsaken Godville to openly challenge the authentic in-residence Levite priest's extensive knowledge or authority, or lack thereof.*

Nor charmer' *leading a virtual charmed life,* nor any one that consulteth *venomous* pythonic spirits, *or vile cobra snakes, or even donkey-cart windshield vipers,* or fortune *or bank* tellers, or *those gone-astray Israelites that undertake* seeking the *morbid* truth from *conversing with* the dead. For the Lord abhorreth all these *diabolical* things *and many others that I can't rightly think of just now,* and for these *substantial* abominations He will destroy them at thy coming, *for mass destruction is indeed His favorite avocation.*

Thou shalt be *a* perfect *idiot,* and without *apparent* spot *or freckles* before the Lord thy God. These *destined* nations, whose land thou shalt *soon* possess, *habitually* hearken to soothsayers and diviners: but thou art otherwise instructed by the *official* Lord thy God, *Who in time* will raise-up to thee a PROPHET of thy nation and of thy *breathing* brethren, *other brash fools* like unto me: Him thou shalt hear talk *of Redemption, and of Resurrection and of Salvation, but unfortunately fellow Israelites, we'll all undoubtedly be long-dead and consequently excluded from ever enjoying those very illuminating future promises and teachings.*

As thou desiredst of the Lord thy God in Horeb, *where Almighty Lord wanted to go tell it on the mountain,* when the assembly was gathered together, *but only I (hoary Moses) had heard Him vociferate.* And He *strangely* saidst *to the apathetic multitude assembled:* "Let Me not hear any more the *booming* Voice of the Lord my God, neither let Me see any more this exceeding great fire, lest I die." I then *pondered and* thought to myself, *"What the hell would happen to me (Moses) and my quixotic dreams of conquest and dominion should the bored moody Lord God suddenly tire of living and then decide to unilaterally extinguish Himself? This is really dangerous shit I'm now contemplating!"*

And the *fiery* Lord said to me *from inside the billowing bush blaze:* "They have spoken all things well. *The talented Israelites are now ready to follow your leadership and sufficiently support you Moses. In the future,* I will raise them up a *superb* prophet out of the midst of their brethren like to thee, *but much greater and more powerful than you presently are:* and I will put my *glorious* words in His mouth, and He shall speak to them *(future Israelites around fifteen hundred years later),* all that I shall command Him *to utter. Is that mystifying concept perfectly clear to you?"*

And he *(the average Joe Israelite)* that will not hear His *stellar* words, which he *(Joe Israelite)* shall speak in My' name, I will be *both* the revenger *and the avenger.* But the *other false anonymous* prophet, who being corrupted with pride *and sinful Gay PRIDE Parades,* shall speak in my *(Moses)* name things that I did not command him to say, or in the name of strange gods, *so in sooth, then the false phony soothsayer shall be viciously* slain *the quickest means possible.*

And if in silent thought thou answer: "How shall I know the word that the *chatterbox* Lord hath not spoken?" Thou shalt have this *logical non-zodiac* sign *to rationally interpret:* Whatsoever that same *pretentious pugnacious prevaricating* prophet *impostor* foretelleth in the name of the Lord *so that the lying augur might realistically profit,* and it cometh not to pass: that thing the Lord hath not spoken, but the *counterfeit* prophet hath forged it by the pride of his *gay-tolerant liberal* mind: and therefore thou shalt not fear him, *but instead, impetuously stone the dastardly charlatan to death before the dumb shit ever gains any dimwitted LBTG converts originating from amongst your rank ranks.*

Chapter Nineteen

"Cities of Refuge"

I estimate that five centuries or so from now, man will have developed quality alphabets and will have the ability to finally chronicle and accurately document history. And I hope and wish that vocabularies will expand and mature and that dictionaries and thesauruses will eventually be carefully organized. Then maybe mankind's suspect thinking will improve also, and future writers will not have to be as stupidly redundant and repetitious as I am being at this very frustrating moment. I greatly fear that these incredible truths I'm vainly attempting to orally express will be grossly distorted by being passed on from generation-to-generation by inefficient word of mouth over the centuries until actual alphabets and corresponding sophisticated written language gradually and thankfully appear on the extremely turmoil-oriented world scene.

The cities of refuge, *where illegal aliens and pugnacious pagans are not tolerated, or welcome, or given haven or sanctuary, for only the appointed illiterate Levite priests are given sanctuaries.* Willful murder and false witnesses must *always* be *fiercely* punished, *just to show the highly ignorant immoral population (including the "who-gives-a-shit" masses) that our religious government theocracy is no more civilized or no more advanced than the average Israelite criminal element is.*

When the Lord thy God hath destroyed the *Un-United nations,* whose *vanquished* land He will deliver to thee *via UUPS (Ubiquitous Utopian Postal System),* and thou shalt possess it *(the monotonously mentioned captured pagan land),* and shalt dwell in the *shoddy* cities, *barrios, slums, ghettos and manifold urban houses thereof:* Thou shalt separate to thee three *important* cities in the midst of the *confiscated* land, *which the Lord will give thee in possession, namely Godville, secondly, God City and thirdly, Metropolitan Godville Megalopolis.*

Paving diligently the way *without knowing one iota about road materials such as tar and asphalt:* and thou shalt divide the whole province of thy land equally into three *distinct* parts, *all the various parts and roles to be enacted and performed upon the phenomenal*

Lord's World Stage: that he who is forced to flee *his cozy residence* for *alleged* manslaughter, *or maybe even for accused woman-slaughter,* may have near at hand whither to escape. *So says my, er, I mean the Lord's new law.*

This shall be the *lucid* law of the *ambitious* slayer that fleeth, *the lucky fugitive from religious justice whose mediocre life is to be saved:* He that killeth his *ignorant* neighbor ignorantly, and who is proved *by a jurisdiction judge or priest* to have had no hatred against him *(his dead victim)* yesterday and the day before: *this very reasonable pre-emptive premeditated killing must be legally allowed, principally, obviously and plausibly because the weirdo ignorant neighbor had all-along been surreptitiously plotting to savagely kill the innocent on-the-lam fugitive from religious justice frantically, riding away from town on the other neighbor's stolen lamb.*

But to have gone with him to the *nearby* wood to hew *and chop* wood, and in cutting down the tree, the *sharp* axe slipped out of his hand, and the iron slipping from the handle struck his *fucked-up* friend, *who had been flagrantly jerking-off under the chopped tree, and the axe's blow inadvertently* killed him *(the self-indulgent bastard) before he could ever achieve a decent climax:* he *(the un-remorseful killer who had been scheming to dispose of his jerk-off hedonistic friend anyway)* shall flee to one of the cities *of refuge* aforesaid, and live there *to make new jerk-off friends to eventually murder.*

Lest perhaps the next kinsman of him *(the murdered jerk-off victim)* whose blood was shed, pushed-on by his grief should pursue, and *ultimately* apprehend him *(the jerk-off murderer),* if the way be too long, and take away the life of him *(who probably is a jerk-off himself)* who is not guilty of death, *accidentally killing another jerk-off,* because he is proved to have had no hatred *or token animosity* before against him that was slain *while being totally preoccupied under the tree rapidly jerking-off.*

Therefore I *(Moses)* command thee *inferior Israelites,* that thou separate *these already-mentioned* three cities at equal distance, one from another. *Namely: Godville, God City and Metropolitan God Megalopolis.* And when the Lord thy God shall have enlarged thy *poorest of porous* borders, *allowing illegal aliens easy access and entrance,* as He swore to the *three dead now-impotent* fathers, and shall give thee all the land that He *had obstinately* promised them *(Abraham, Isaac and Jacob and not Abraham, Martin and John), that is, after the all-too-familiar encroached-upon territory is sufficiently invaded, adroitly conquered and then subsequently confiscated.*

(Yet so, if thou keep his Ten Commandments, and do the *basic* things which I command thee this day, that thou love the Lord thy God, and walk in His ways at all times), *although none of us irrelevant dopes seem to ever know His mysterious whereabouts.* Thou shalt add to the other three cities, and shalt double the number of the three cities aforesaid: *Consider establishing terrific places like Mosesville, Moses Town and Mosesburg.*

That innocent blood may not be shed in the midst of the land which the Lord thy God will give thee to possess, lest thou be guilty of blood, *and if so, then you'll become a blood brother to the axe-wielding jerk-off who had brutally killed his friend (the other jerk-off) who had been accidentally slaughtered while eagerly jerking-off under the tall shade tree.*

But if any man hating his neighbor *(perhaps a Mr. Rogers type, for instance),* lie in wait for his life, and rise and strike him *with the said tree axe weapon,* and he *(the new jerk-off guy)* dies, and he *(the new jerk-off murderer)* flees to one of the *new-found* cities aforesaid, then the senile ancients of his *new* city shall send *their wrinkled wives as soldiers* and take him out of the place of refuge, and shall deliver him *(the new jerk-off murderer who has been professionally apprehended by the recently deputized wrinkled old bitches)* into the hand of the kinsman of him whose blood was shed, and he shall die by *excruciating assassination just like any wanton craven coward ought to perish.*

Thou shalt not pity him, and thou shalt take away the guilt of innocent blood out of Israel, that it may be well with thee, because we don't *need bad blood to perform dangerous medical transfusions in inhospitable hospital tents, even the few successful blood replacement operations that are performed by the lunatic rabid rabbi doctors who specialize in doing gruesome circumcisions and other approved forms of bizarre body mutilation.*

Thou shalt not take nor remove thy neighbor's landmark *fences, garages, outhouses, smoke-houses, marijuana smoke-houses, storage sheds, trash bins or accessible random port-a-potties* which thy *irresponsible* predecessors have set in thy possession, which the Lord thy God will *gladly* give thee in the *pilfered* land that thou shalt receive to possess.

One witness shall not rise up against any man, *especially if he claims to be a bona-fide Jehovah Witness, for I (Moses) am the only reliable Jehovah Witness allowed anywhere in Godville or, for that matter, permitted to interpret the Lord's indispensable message anywhere in Israel Proper.* Whatsoever the sin or wickedness be: but in the mouth of two *or three non-Jehovah witnesses,* every *legitimate* word shall stand *until their overcrowded mouths have standing word only status.*

If a lying witness *(erect on his feet and not lying prone on the ground)* stand against a *leaning* man, accusing him of transgression, both of them (the two standing fools), between whom the controversy is, shall stand *or lean* before the Lord in the sight of the *senile demented* priests and the *palsied ancient judges* that shall be *in power during* those *alluded to* days. *But when the palsied old senile rabbi on the front lines yells-out the following inspiring words, "Priesto-change-o!," that's the magical religious cue that dramatically signals we staunch Israelites to urgently advance and start aggressively kicking pagan ass.*

And when after most diligent *rhetorical* inquisition, they shall find that the false witness hath told a *deceitful treacherous* lie against his *fucked-up* brother: They *(the geriatric judge and priest)* shall render to him as he meant to do to his brother, and thou *(the public)* shalt take away the evil out of the midst of thee *and beat the living and digested feces out of the unscrupulous false testifier.*

That others hearing may fear *having the smelly shit beaten out of them and then having to eat and devour their own excrement too,* and may not dare to do such *similar fucked-up things like bearing false witness ever again, for many of those cocky deleterious assholes would rather eat crow than be forced under penalty of death to swallow-down their own putrid diarrhea crap.*

Thou shalt not pity him *(the diabolical false accuser),* but shalt require life for life, eye for an eye, tooth for a tooth, hand for hand, foot for a foot, *dick for a dick, or possibly five pieces of silver for a good personalized pussy screw or chew, or perhaps for a decent customized super blow-job.*

Chapter Twenty

"Courage in War"

These are the Laws relating to war, *either civilized or uncivilized conflicts.* If thou go out to war against *thy close friends* or thy *close-by* enemies, and see *bevies of approaching* horsemen and chariots *of fire,* and the numbers of the *strong* enemy's army greater than thine *disorganized platoon,* thou shalt not fear them: because the Lord thy God is *indeed* with thee, Who *intrepidly* brought thee out of the land of Egypt *for the purpose of small platoons to courageously do battle with huge overwhelming armies.*

And when the *significant* battle is now at hand, the cowardly priest, *who is afraid of either his own or your shadow,* shall stand before the *disheveled Hebrew* army, *perform some elementary shadow boxing maneuvers,* and then the *weak feckless dolt* shall speak to the people *(amateur men, women and children platoon soldiers)* in this *queer* manner: "Hear, O Israel, *the only nation on Earth with donkey ears,* you join battle this *accursed* day against your *myriad* enemies, *that together constitute the remainder of the known world's civilized population.* Let not your *dismal* hearts be dismayed; be not afraid, do not give back, fear ye them not, *even if their weapons are made out of bronze and iron and ours out of flimsy balsa wood and imported flaccid bamboo.*

Because *certainly* the *invisible* Lord your God is in the midst of you, and *He* will *fiercely* fight for you against your *infinite avowed* enemies, to deliver you from *impending evil, but obviously not from imminent danger.*

And the captains shall meet *for the opening coin toss* and then proclaim through every *musical rock or rap* band in the hearing *range* of the *disorganized* army: "What man is there, that hath built a new house, and hath not dedicated it *to a fucked-up religious cause such as ours?* Let him go and return to his *fucked-up* house, lest he *futilely* dies in the *about-to-occur* battle, and another man dedicates it to *his own fucked-up non-religious cause. Listen to me and to my questionable absurd rhetoric, you ungrateful quacks, and learn not esoteric wisdom!"*

"What *impractical* man is there, that hath planted *watermelons and giant squashes and saguaro cactus in the precise middle of a* vineyard, and the *quixotic fool* hath not as yet made it *(the garden exotic vineyard)* to be *producing* common *food,* whereof all *silly* men may eat and drink *at the defunct community wine garden?* Let him *(the friendly Israelite coward)* go, and *speedily* return to his *shabby shoddy rock* house *or tattered desert tent with the big expensive two-tone donkey cart parked outside,* lest he *needlessly* dies in the *wicked* slaughter, and another *avaricious* Hebrew man *moves-in and* executes his office *and greedily steals his former properties, his girlfriends, his commodious toilet, his concubines, and his wives."*

What man is there, that hath espoused a *rare virgin* wife, and not taken her *firm ass onto a soft haystack for erect penis pumping?* Let him go, and return to his *indigenous* house, lest he die in the *brutal imaginary theoretical* war, and another *impulsive* man take her *(the broken-in toilet-trained dependent hussy) and then the happy husband substitute vigorously and literally pumps the poop out of the horny kinky bitch, screwing both his and her asses right off the soft haystack's pinnacle.*

After these *weird and strange* things are declared *and confirmed (but not Baptized) to be fundamentally true and accurate,* they shall add the rest, and shall speak *forcefully* to the *indolent who-gives-a-shit grumbling assembled* people: "What man is there that is fearful *and ball-less,* and faint hearted *after suffering castration and severe strokes?* Let him go, and return to his *abandoned* house *(shack, shanty),* lest he make the hearts of his *wimpy* brethren to fear *also,* as he himself is *grossly* possessed with fear, *and then before we will even know it, all of Israel, even our adventurous mariner seamen, will have no balls or vital spermatozoa fluid left!*

And when the *spineless* captains of the army *refuse to participate in the pre-battle coin toss, they* shall hold their peace *along with their drooping testicles,* and have made an end of speaking *sanctimonious cowardly bullshit,* every man shall *use reverse war psychology* and prepare their rock *(throwing)* bands to fight *to the bitter end. It is always better to retreat from battle than to surrender and be fuckin' decapitated. Even a complete dumb asshole like me (Moses) understands this wise principle. I mean in essence, how much more rudimentary can basic logic get?*

If at any time thou come to fight against a *large* city *having brave warriors,* thou shalt first offer it *fraudulent* peace, *because if a mentally deficient Israelite man wants to alone fight an entire maniacal city, then he's so fucked-up that the dumb-ass fuck-head deserves to get viciously sodomized over and over again and then wickedly castrated too.*

If they *(the pagan enemy?)* receive it, and open the *flood* gates to thee, all the people that are therein, shall be saved *from drowning,* and shall serve thee paying tribute *and promoting thee to the non-influential low rank of "Shallow Water Lifeguard."* But if they *(the unappreciative city pagan beach bums)* will not *take the initiative to* make peace, and shall begin *administering turbulent* war against thee, thou shalt besiege it *and proceed to drown all of the dumb-shit assholes in either the big adult swimming pool or in the nearby kiddy wading cesspool.*

And when the Lord thy God shall deliver it *(vital first aid kits and scalpels)* into thy *fleeing paramedics'* hands, thou shalt use t*he new-found items* to slay all that are therein of the male sex, with the *sharp* edge of the *hand* sword *pointing squarely at their exposed testicles. But beware of a possible precarious situation defiant Israelite: if the intended victim is a wily trans-gender transvestite, he or she might not be able to be immediately identified as being either a fucked-up male or a fucked-up female to be castrated.*

Excepting *contingents of reserve soldiers that are* women and children, cattle and other *relevant* things *(I guess you thought that women and children were people as opposed to being things), that are desperately prowling around and scavenging for food morsels in the pagan city trash heap, here is the best solution to drastically implement.* Thou shalt divide all the prey to thy *accompanying* army, and thou shalt eat the spoils of thy enemies *before ravenously eating the recognized enemies from the head down, of* which the Lord thy God shall give thee *on bamboo and balsa wood platters. All of this I (Moses) sagely predict will happen. Matters are quite easy to decipher when my superior mind effectively utilizes simple cause and effect reasoning.*

So shalt thou do to *all the pagan disease infested and infected* cities that are *hypothetically* at a great distance from thee, and are not of these *other conquered* cities which thou shalt receive in possession *for achieving a great military victory by means of us' cleverly employing the technique of shrewd military trickery. The accomplishment will be as easy as kosher bagels!*

But of those *captured* cities that shall be *reluctantly* given thee *in this marvelous Old Testament Bible Monopoly Game,* thou shalt suffer *no major injury* at all to live *and endure after you have passed "Go!"* But *thou* shalt kill them all *(the evil pagan donkey cart gang members) on the Boardwalk or on the Park Place square* with the *honed blade* edge of the *razor-sharp scalpel* sword, to wit, the Hethite, and the *amorous* Amorrhite, and the *cannibalistic* Canaanite, the *parasitic* Pherezite, and the *heinous* Hevite, and the Jebusite, and the *Jeb-Bushite too, and finally, the tricky and coy Atlanticcityite,* as the Lord thy God hath *imperially* commanded thee *to exterminate. And furthermore, while you're at it, kill all the fucked-up parsimonious Anacinites too before those bellicose barbarian bastards give you terrible my-groin headaches! If not done right away, they'll surely singe your rectum until your bare ass burns!"*

Lest they *(the fucked-up infidel pagans)* teach you to do all the abominations which they have done to their *molten lava-assed* gods: and you should *grievously* sin against the Lord your God, *be content that you have effectively eliminated the remainder of the hideous insidious pagans, for they are a direct menace to our society and to our inferior culture and religion.*

When thou hast besieged a *pagan* city *for* a long time, and hath compassed and *compressed* it with bulwarks *and working bulls that are not dozing,* to take it *completely,* thou shalt not cut-down the trees that may be eaten of *delicious fruit, and* neither shalt thou spoil the country round about *and the donkey cart roundabouts with tree-barking* axes: for it is a *wonderful dogwood* tree, and not a man *or woman,* neither can it *(the barking dogwood tree or the personified barking axe, reader take your pick)* increase the number of them *(dumb-shit pagans)* that fight against thee. *This salient fact (I maintain) is an indisputable gospel truth!*

But if there be any trees that are not fruitful, but *strangely growing* wild *vegetables instead,* and fit for other uses, *certainly* cut them down, and *use the acquired materials to* make *climbing and boarding ramparts'* engines, until thou take the city, which fighteth against thee *(along with the pernicious pagan occupants), because the shifty heathen enemy might have some stealthy branch offices concealed inside the sinister dogwood tree forest that might be surrounding the pagan city. Indeed, my principal responsibility is to always make common sense out of extraneous Biblical nonsense!*

Chapter Twenty-one

"Expiation of Untraced Murder"

The expiation of a secret murder *could represent a difficult cult conundrum to first analyze and then systematically resolve.* The marrying of a captive *could be a real moral challenge, with the Hebrew captor and the pagan captive both living inside a small cellar cage together.* The eldest son must not be deprived of his birthright (*or his blotchy birth-mark*) for hatred of his *heathen* mother, *and the jaded son may even then call his derelict father a "pagan mother-fucker."* A stubborn son is to be stoned to death *with a heavy barrage of hot volcanic rocks. But* when the *wise-assed little prick* is *justifiably* hanged *by his balls* on a gibbet, he must be taken down the same day and *immediately* buried *in squalor with his abused crushed testicles still intact; otherwise, the failed executioner is then subsequently hanged by his testicles on the dreaded public gibbet in a similar humiliating manner.*

When there shall be found in the land, which the Lord thy God will give *generously to* thee, the corpse of a man slain, *and I've perceptively noticed that these numerous annoying cadavers are casually strewn all over the fuckin' place,* and it is not known who is guilty of *committing* the *alleged* murder, then thy *senile geriatric* ancients and *thy forgetful* judges shall go out, and shall measure from the place where the body lieth the distance of every city round about, *in order to estimate and determine the appropriate geographic coordinates in relation to the general position of the setting sun, but I (Moses) must confess that this beleaguering enterprise is an exceptionally tough assignment when performed on a cloudy, overcast, rainy day.*

And the *enfeebled diaper-wearing* ancients of that *dilapidated* city which they shall perceive to be nearer than the rest *of the other area metropolitan dumps,* shall take a *sturdy virile* heifer of the herd, that hath not drawn in the yoke *and that most closely resembles a fat pagan prostitute,* nor has *the selected female-faced heifer ever* ploughed the ground, and they shall bring her *(the heifer that looks like a fat pagan female)* into a rough and stony valley, that never was ploughed nor sown *by any available animal, either male or female,* and there *in that extremely propitious place* they shall strike-off the

119

ugly head of the heifer *to religiously purify the remote desolate desert valley.*

And the *palsied* priests, the *unpredictable* sons of the *not-too-cerebral* Levi *blue canvas makers,* shall come, whom the Lord thy God hath *expressly* chosen to minister to Him *and satisfy His myriad bizarre whims,* and to bless *ugly pagan-looking heifer heads* in His *sacred* name, and that by their word *(the fucked-up denim-vested illiterate Levi priests),* every matter, *even some anti-matter,* should be decided, and whatsoever is clean or unclean should be judged by the *belligerent* Levi *priests during local afternoon infertile valley melodramatic soap operas, ordinarily attended by no one.*

And the *piss-their-robes* ancients of that *plagued anonymous* city shall come to the person slain, and shall wash their hands over the *mutilated* heifer that was killed (slaughtered) *in the arid Hebrew valley and not in Cow-cutta! Such is the grand sagacity of our imbecilic laws and fucked-up regulations.*

And shall the *mentally challenged* Levi *priests all* say *in unison:* "Our *filthy callused* hands did not shed this blood, nor did our eyes see it. *If we vigorously wipe our irises, we shall then all have bloodshot eyes!"*

Be merciful to thy people Israel, whom Thou hast in the past *seen fit to have* redeemed *for food stamps in the form of Manna from Heaven,* O Lord, and lay not innocent blood *to be deposited* into their *bankrupt* charge *accounts,* in the midst of thy' *who-cares-a-crap invading* people, *namely* Israel. And the guilt of blood shall be taken from them *before they abandon me (Moses) and the selfsame pathetic apathetic Israelites, through their devious antics and semantics, then adapt and learn to solicit the indispensable services of skillful urban pagan psychiatrists.*

And thou shalt be free from the innocent's blood, that was shed *near the Israelite army's bustling refreshment shed,* when thou shalt have done what the Lord hath commanded thee *to do, and promptly stick the bloody heifer's bony head onto thine' own. Such is the will of the Lord!*

If thou go out to fight against thy *countless* enemies, and the Lord thy God *shrink them down and* deliver them into thy *gigantic* hand, and thou lead them away as *unhappy camper* captives, *then as a reward you'll be entitled to free beer and wine at the all-too-busy military refreshment concession.*

And seest in the number of the captives a beautiful woman *with big hard knockers and huge suckable brown nipples,* and lovest her *with your commendable aroused hard-on,* and wilt have her to wife, *to love, honor and screw five times daily. Then* thou shalt bring her into thy *grotesque-looking tawdry* house, *awkwardly carrying her fine tight ass through the closed window threshold:* and she shall *cooperatively* shave her *pussy* and *armpit* hair *also,* and pare her nails *so that she may scratch your hairy pimply ass on demand while having mutual hot heterosexual intercourse.*

And thou shall put off the clothes, wherein she was taken: and thou shall remain in thy house *stark naked,* and mourn for her *dead* father and mother *(that thou had conveniently killed)* one month *earlier, until she again gets her periodic period: and after that bloody mess, which very much resembles the hideous slaughtering of the beheaded heifer,* thou shalt go in unto her *snatcheroo,* and shalt *comfortably* sleep with her, and she shall be thy *humping and pumping* wife *until the dead heifers comes home.*

But if afterwards she please thee not, *complaining of dubious my-groin headaches, back aches, and also bitching about other stupid bullshit like that,* thou shalt let her go free, but thou mayst not sell her for money nor oppress her by might because thou hast *already* humbled *and screwed* her, *and therefore, your intended profitable pimping of her useless frigid snatcheroo is now totally forbidden, according to the law.*

If a man have two *or more* wives, one beloved, and the other hated, and they have had *bratty* children by him, *both bitches sharing his fertile seeds,* and the son of the hated be the firstborn, *and if said firstborn's face looks something like a chicken's countenance, then thou has acted like a kinky rooster and thou lout has been screwing around with the hens' eggs and with the hens' ovaries in the backyard capon coop.*

121

And he *(the triumphant-but-unhappy Israelite)* meaneth to divide his substances *(drugs and marijuana)* among his *impudent* sons: he may not make the *chicken-looking* son of the beloved the firstborn, and prefer him before the *rooster-looking* son of the hated *wife. That's precisely what the hell horny chicken hens' think and blithely say: "Cock-a-doodle-do; any cock'll do!"*

But he *(the perplexed and sexually frustrated Israelite)* shall *eventually* acknowledge the son of the hated for the firstborn, *that might in fact be the worst born also,* and shall give him a double portion of all he hath *accumulated: brashly telling the brazen juvenile punk, "Double on nothing, Asshole!"* for this is the first *and worst* of his *insolent* children, and to him *(the beleaguered Israelite husband/father's second asshole son)* is due the first *son's formerly privileged* birthrights, *to be soon followed by the younger jerk-off's absolute and final Last Rites and burial!*

If a man have a stubborn and unruly son, who will not hear *or listen to* the *arbitrary* commandments of his father or *his pagan-minded* mother, and *after* being corrected *and reprimanded,* slighteth obedience, *yelling back embarrassing expletives like "Fuck off!" and "Fuck you!"* well, then *the fed-up parents* shall take him *(the nasty punk asshole kid)* and bring him to the *senile* ancients of the *nearby licentious* city, and *escort the abusive juvenile delinquent shithead* to the gate of judgment *where the incorrigible thuggish kid will be violently flogged until his foul mouth begins to actively shit green piss.*

And *thou* shall say to them *(the fucked-up elders):* "This our *fucked-up* son is *defiantly* rebellious and stubborn; he slighteth hearing our *bullshit* admonitions, he giveth himself to reveling *with my adult girlfriends and sensual consensual couch dancers, and the punk asshole dares to barbarically practice debaucherous, scurrilous sex on the head tables at distinguished wedding banquets, at formal bar-mitzvahs, and at solemn funerals."*

The *derelict* people of the city shall *automatically* stone him, *the irresponsible juvenile delinquent jerk-off:* and he shall die *later from frostbite, malnutrition and from an austere protein-less vegan diet,* that you may then take away the evil demon out of the midst of you, and all Israel hearing it may be *immensely* afraid *of frostbite, of malnutrition symptoms, and of repulsive protein-less austere vegan diets.*

Finally dear beloved brethren, when a man hath committed a *horrible* crime for which he is to be punished with *dishonorable* death, and being condemned to die is *naturally* to be hanged on a gibbet: His body *(the former swinger's and now the main gallows' swinger's)* shall not remain upon the tree, but *instead the noose-ance* shall be buried the same day *into a stinking community cesspool:* for he' is cursed by God, *the dead sinner* that hangeth on a *dead deciduous* tree: and thou shalt not defile thy *stolen* land, which the Lord thy God shall give thee in possession *in exchange for your solicited ungrateful half-hearted allegiance.*

Chapter Twenty-two

"Care for Lost Animals"

This statement is about humanity towards neighbors, *especially the sex-starved next door wives having big hard boobs and hairy hungry crotches.* Neither sex' may use the apparel of the other and cruelty is to be avoided, even to birds, *including your own red throbbing non-wood pecker. But* the punishment of him that slandereth his *obese flabby titted wife,* as also of adultery and rape, *and such bullshit bedroom activity will quickly get your privileged ass sent back to the Egyptian S and M Bondage and Mutilation Clinic in metropolitan downtown Cairo.*

Thou shalt not pass by if thou seest thy brother's ox, cow or his sheep go astray: but thou shalt bring them back to thy brother *so that you can easily and readily pick-pocket his wallet while the oblivious trustworthy gullible imbecile is preoccupied bent over utterly examining his lost cow's udders.*

And if thy brother be not nigh, or thou know him not: thou shalt bring them to thy house, and they shall be with thee until thy brother seek them, and receive them. *And after thy anonymous brother makes passes at or screws your promiscuous wife in either a private or a public place, then frenetically beat the crap and piss out of him and next boot his arrogant haughty ass right out the only filthy window in your crude rock house or right out of your flimsy rotting tent.*

Thou shalt do in like manner with his ass, and with his raiment *(clothes),* and with everything' that is thy brother's, which' is lost: if thou find it, neglect it not as pertaining to another. *But remember to now beat the digested and the un-digested crap out of the anonymous flirting gigolo brother every single freakin' time you see the bastard conniving around the squeaky back doors of your vulnerable neighborhood. Community watch along with personal vigilance is always recommended in order to guard your horny promiscuous wife from being advantageously screwed by total strangers.*

If thou see thy brother's ass or his ox to be fallen down in the way, thou shalt not slight it, but shalt lift it up with him *off his own ass, and then kick both his asses, that is to say, the despicable two-faced, two-assed asshole anonymous brother.*

A woman shall not be clothed with man's apparel, neither shall a man use woman's apparel, *unless of course they be registered as legitimate trans-gender transvestites with the senile priests and rabbis living together as humble hermits at the always-empty downtown synagogue*: for he that doth these things is abominable before God, *who positively loathes trans-gender transvestites along with senile elders, judges and assorted prophets, that is, all except me (Marvelous Moses).*

If thou find as thou walkest by the way *to the local brothel*, a bird's nest in a tree, or on the ground, and the dam sitting upon the young or upon the *un-hatched* eggs: thou shalt not take her with her young *born or unborn: or else as the Lord had frequently told me, "The yolk's on you all the way to the freakin' weed-infested cemetery. No Heaven for you or for your pathetic mentally challenged Israelites, Moses!"*

But *in regard to animals other than the standard birds and the bees,* shalt let her *(the mother bird bitch)* go, keeping the young which thou hast caught *to feed to your famished cat or pet lion:* that it may be well with thee, and thou mayst live a long time, *also dutifully feeding your wife's furry cat to your heart's and your balls content.*

When thou buildest a *new modern rock* home *featuring a two-seat inside outhouse*, thou shalt make a battlement to the roof round about *to protect you and your wife while you're taking dual shits:* lest blood be shed in thy house *from both of your exposed assholes,* and thou be *judged* guilty *for your negligence; that is,* if anyone slips, and falls down headlong *from the accumulated crap lying on the cruddy wood floor. And in regard to* battlements: This precaution was necessary because all the rudely constructed Israelite houses have flat tops, and it was usual to walk and to converse together upon them *(the roofs) while the pagan enemy would be ambitiously climbing the low outside walls with their makeshift ladders to attack and kill the nonchalant strolling Jewish occupants, most of them anyway seeking a quick death and instant escape from the Lord's cruel everyday Promised Land reality.*

126

Thou shalt not sow thy vineyard with divers *(or lady cadavers')* seeds: lest both the seed which thou hast sown, and the fruit of the vineyard, be sanctified together *by the senile palsied rabbis' blessing, the dedicated elders also being afflicted with something basically mysterious and ominous that's now medically called Parkinson's.*

Thou shalt not plough with an ox and an ass together, *you horse's ass.* And thou shalt not wear a garment that is woven of woolen and linen together, *or you my dear precious Israelite might still think you're home sleeping in bed. And too,* thou shalt make strings in the hem at the four corners of thy cloak, wherewith thou shalt be covered when *walking around cavorting in public, with all worn material publicly showing above thy silly-looking bouncing genitals.*

If a man marries a wife, *either male or female,* and afterwards hates her, *either male or female,* and seeks occasions to put her away *in a cheap mental institution located in the root cellar of the senile rabbi's partially collapsed synagogue, the disgruntled husband* charging her with a very ill name *like "bitch," or "whore," or "harlot,"* and *then* sayeth *to the rabbi who had chronically screwed the unfaithful wife ever since she had entered puberty in first semester kindergarten:* "I took this woman to be *my lawful wedded* wife, and going into her, I found her not a virgin, *but instead, rather her being an old used common community slut!"*

"Her father and mother shall take her," *the rabbi explains with a broad smile,* "and they shall bring with them the tokens of her virginity to the *erudite* ancients of the city *that are vigorously smoking marijuana joints in* the gate. *Yes indeed, those old abstinent bastards know everything about everything!"*

And the *ashamed* father shall say *and insist to the mentally ill rabbi:* "I gave my daughter unto this man to wife: *and because he hateth her, she became pissed-off at her louse of a spouse and then spitefully stuck an oversized cucumber directly up into her undersized snatcheroo! That's precisely how the horny bitch lost her fragile virginity!"*

He *(watch with the rampant pronoun-noun-antecedent problem, will you please? "He" is the disenchanted husband)* layeth to her

127

charge a very ill name, so as to say: "I found not thy daughter a pure virgin: and behold these are the tokens of my daughter's virginity:" *a moth-eaten bra and a red-stained unsanitary napkin!* And they shall spread the cloth before the ancients of the city *so that the old-time geezers puffing away on their reefer joints (and sometimes on each other's limp joints) can each smell the woman's (the daughter's) red-stained rag and then render a fair and just determination.*

And the *profound* ancients of that *fucked-up* city shall take that man *(the indignant husband), and using large clubs,* beat him *to a pulp because they too had merrily screwed the accused adulterous wife when they each were merely eighty-eight years old (young).*

Condemning him *(the appalled insulted husband)* besides in a hundred bits of silver, which he shall *reluctantly* give to the damsel's *shrewd* father, *who makes extra cash as her (his daughter's) wealthy pimp,* because he *(the appreciative pimp's offended son-in-law)* hath defamed by a very ill name a *virtuous* virgin of Israel: and *sexually frustrated* he *(the pissed-off husband antagonist)* shall *again* have her *(his exonerated spouse)* to wife, and he may not put her away *into the senile rabbi's gravel-floored root cellar* all the *remaining* days of his life.

But if what he *(the fit-to-be-tied husband)* charged her with be true, and virginity be not found in the damsel: They *(the feeble-minded doddering city elders)* shall cast her out of the doors of her father's house, and the men of the city shall *wildly* stone her to death, and she shall die: *but in all candor, this scenario will never happen because the all-too-shrewd accused wife will naturally indict and prosecute the entire adult male population of the sinful city because both* she *and they* hath done a wicked thing in Israel, to play being the whore in her father's house: and thou shalt take away the evil out of the midst of the town *by then re-circumcising all the stoned city elders if the wily connivers are ultimately found guilty of collusion by me, Prophet Moses.*

If a man' lie *(or tell the truth)* with another man's wife, they shall both die, that is to say, the adulterer and the adulteress: and thou shalt take away the evil out of Israel. *This particular law had been originally written by me (Meticulous Moses) along with the powerful Undertakers' and Body Embalmers Union.*

If a man have espoused a damsel *(in distress with her period)* that is a *bloody* virgin, and some one finds her in the city *screwing around on top of a popular highly frequented haystack,* and lie with her, *then* Thou shalt bring them both out to the gate of that city, and they shall be stoned *by the already stoned elders:* the damsel *in this dress,* because she cried not out *while being raped or while having her pleasurable orgasm, or while being improperly laid and porked* in the city *proper:* the *sex-crazed* man, because he hath humbled his *sex-crazed* neighbor's *sex-crazed* wife, *shall be mercilessly killed without regular prosecution.* And thou *(jilted husband)* take away the evil from the midst of thee *by next becoming permanently abstinent and celibate, qualifying thee (the totally peeved male spouse) to become a senile community elder seventy years hence down the road.*

But if a man *with a decent erection* finds a *fairly fair* damsel that is betrothed, *and she is viewed privately masturbating like crazy* in the *adjacent* field, and taking hold of her hand *and then climbing atop the popular village haystack to wildly hump and pump her into sensational ecstasy,* and *then* lie with her *after getting caught by the young girl's father, the strict farmer owning the popular village haystack,* he *(the now-sperm-less asshole no longer having the huge erection)* alone shall die.

And the *sexually satisfied* damsel shall suffer nothing *but gratifying pleasure,* and neither is she guilty of death: for as a robber riseth against his brother *to engage in sodomy,* and taketh away his life *by screwing his brother's asshole to death,* so also did the damsel suffer *mental anguish. But in truth, the sexually relieved damsel was much smarter than the asshole sodomy brothers since she had been intelligent enough to realize that an asshole is an exit; whereas, a wet pink vagina is an accommodating convenient entrance.*

She was alone in the field: she cried, and there was no man to help her *attain orgasm, so the damsel had to resort to ordinary clit-rubbing masturbation.* If a man finds a *gorgeous* damsel *exuberantly masturbating like crazy in a field or haystack,* and suspects that she is a *horny* virgin, who is not espoused to another *jerk-off,* and *then* taking her, lie with her *and gets his middle finger nice and wet,* and the *delicate* matter comes to the *senile elders' attention and* judgment: He *(the horny jerk-off passing by the familiar, highly frequented haystack or popular masturbating field)* that lay with her shall give to the father of the maid fifty bits of silver *for simply getting his middle finger wet,* and shall have her to wife, because he hath humbled her *with his wet smelly middle finger:* he may not put her away all the days of his life *inside the demented pedophile rabbi's gravel-floored root cellar. In conclusion, no M.F-ing* man shall take his father's wife, nor remove his *(old man's) blanket* covering *while his aroused dad is plowing-away into an appreciative eager beaver upon the master's master bedroom straw-covered, rickety cot.*

Chapter Twenty-three

"Community Membership"

Who may and who may not enter into the *rabbi's dim dank* church *or synagogue:* uncleanness, *dirty underwear, sperm stains, period stains and brown and green shit stains are* to be avoided *by the cautious pedestrian:* other precepts concerning fugitives, *whores,* fornication, *lesbians,* usury, vows, *consonants, vowels, trans-gender transvestites* and eating other men's grapes and corn *or munching on other men's wives hairy pussies shall all be severely punished by austere scripture law.*

An eunuch, whose testicles are broken, *crushed* or cut away, or *his* yard-*long dick* cut off *for public display in the sausage vendor's stall at the city marketplace,* shall not enter into the church of the Lord *until he grows a new set of balls and/or has emergency gender surgery done (by the doddering rabbi and his forgetful priest assistant) upon his abbreviated dick. Listen-up! Rule number one of The Wholly Book of Doo-Doo-Rot-on-Me is: "To be a male Israelite, a guy must first have balls and a functional erect dick too!"*

Eunuch... By these are meant, in the spiritual sense, such as are barren in good works, into the *official* church. *But in truth eunuchs can never be brave Jewish jerk-offs because they have no fuckin' balls to begin jerking-off with, or fundamentally, no viable testicles to facilitate an appropriate orgasm while anxiously jerking-off.* That is *to say,* into the assembly or congregation of *seed-bearing* Israel, so as to have the privilege of *watching* an Israelite *shooting sperm jets into the air or into a receptive lady's hairy pussy,* or to be capable of any place or office among the people of God, *those egotistical sex-hungry debauchers all having a wild Bacchus-type orgy in the naughty rabbi's gravel-floored root cellar should all be violently stoned inside the revered local beer garden.*

A mamzer, that is to say, one born of a prostitute, shall not enter into the church of the Lord, until the tenth generation, *or he being two hundred years old. But at least the mamzer's mother was a professional prostitute and not a practicing whore, for at least prostitutes get paid (for being laid) for their sexual favors and then the pleasure Janes can easily financially support a dysfunctional*

131

lazy mamzer or two, but on the other hand, whores just screw around for fun without receiving any special monetary compensation for their vital service, voluntarily rendered for free to the straight (or gay) community.

The *gruesome* Ammonite and the Moabite *Dickie pagans,* even after the tenth generation, shall not enter into the church of the Lord: they *(those heathen lava-worshiping scumbags)* cannot enter *the portals into the sanctified synagogue until they are at least a mature and fully cleansed four hundred years of age.*

Because they *(the Ammonites and the Moabite Dickies)* would not meet you *(the oppressed Israelites)* with bread and water in the way *from Egypt,* when you *finally* came out of *the* Cairo *S and M Bondage Whorehouse Closet,* they *(the A and M boys, not from Texas)* hired against thee Balaam, the son of Beor, from Mesopotamia in Syria, to *perniciously* curse thee *with a lot of nonsensical pagan religious bullshit.*

And the Lord thy God would not hear Balaam, and He turned his cursing *(Balaam's belligerent bullshit)* into thy blessing, because He loved thee *and not Balaam's fucked-up belligerent bullshit.* Thou shalt not make any peace with them *(the mendacious A and M barbarians who genuinely like and prefer Balaam's blustery belligerent bullshit),* neither shalt thou seek their prosperity all the days of thy life forever, *which will never happen because the Gates of Heaven are tightly closed to the accursed Israelites, and only the jealous Lord and His formidable archangels can meander-around with impunity up in the floating clouds.*

Thou shalt not abhor the Edomite, because he is thy *illegitimate* brother: nor the Egyptian, because thou wast a *perplexed* stranger in his *plagued* land, *so therefore I highly recommend to you, never ever walk like an Egyptian.* They that are born of them *(the Edomites and the Egyptians),* in the third generation shall *be allowed to* enter into the church of the Lord, *but those wily itinerant pagans will never step into the altar zone of our sacred synagogue because the scared stealthy heathens don't give a shit about our primitive Neanderthal-type culture or about our primitive and prehistoric Jewish religion.*

When thou goest out to war against thy enemies, thou shalt keep thyself from every evil thing *that might distract you from killing the foe, or that sideshow might distract you from actually being killed yourself.* If there be among you any *normal* man', that is defiled in a *white* dream by night, he shall go forth out of the camp *because obviously he is then too fuckin' sperm-less to do battle for more than thirty seconds because of his lustful premature ejaculation that he had sinfully experienced in his sleep the night before.*

And *the fatigued disgraced soldier* shall not return *to the bloody battlefield,* before he be washed with water in the evening, *thus essentially rejuvenating his flaccid dick and re-activating his terribly weakened reproductive balls:* and after sunset he *(the sexually relieved shamed soldier)* shall return into the camp, *all ready to already have another white dream in his next restive sleep.*

Thou *(the white dream soldier)* shalt have a place without the camp, to which thou mayst go for the necessities of nature, *so now our Israelite soldiers can freely piss, shit and jerk-off inside the small military pavilion that's been conveniently set-up outside the overcrowded army beer and wine garden refreshment booth.*

Carrying a paddle at thy girdle *to keep the belly-jelly flab inside your loose skirt,* and when thou sittest down, *keep thy legs closed so that other more discreet and moral patrons at the open-air restaurant may not notice your exposed bulging genitals or hear your sustained loud farting.* And then thou shalt dig round about *outside the eatery,* and with the Earth that is dug up, thou shalt *carefully* cover *upon the newly fertilized ground thy recently released fecal matter.*

That which thou art eased of: (for the Lord thy God walketh in the midst of thy *campy* camp, to deliver thee *from nothing,* and to give up thy *evil pagan* enemies to thee (*so that you may go home to your uncomfortable pad and make your girlfriend or unfaithful wife surrender also):* and let thy *entire* camp be *wholly* holy, and let no uncleanness appear therein *in the form of smudgy sperm stains or rather unappealing shit stains,* lest He go away from thee *holding his nose tight, for filth and fecal stench* driveth God away from the *human* soul.

133

Thou shalt not deliver to his master the servant that is fled to thee *so that you then may also abuse the spoiled subordinate in a similar manner as to how his former gay boss had molested and sodomized the disobedient fucked-up asshole.* He *(the on-the-lam sodomized apprehensive servant)* shall dwell with thee in the place that shall please him, and shall rest in one of thy cities *you had acquired by playing the boring Hebrew Monopoly Game for Beginners,* so for *the first week,* give him *(the sodomized fleeing apprehensive paranoid servant) no particular* trouble.

There shall be no whore among the daughters of Israel, nor whoremonger among the sons of Israel. *There shall only be money-taking capitalistic prostitutes legally working in licensed brothels and in bona fide government-sanctioned bordellos. And let there be no geld disseminated for gelding male transvestite trans-gender whores either!*

Thou shalt not offer the hire of a strumpet, *whether she (the audacious harlot bitch) plays the trumpet or the proverbial skin flute or not,* nor pay the price of a dog *for sale,* in the house of the Lord thy God, whatsoever it be that thou hast vowed *to either whores or prostitutes,* because both these *disreputable classifications* are an abomination to the Lord thy God *and to me Moses also, but the grateful synagogue rabbis and priests both receive under-the-table handsome commissions from the working prostitutes, but conversely, the Holy Men do not obtain one cheap copper coin from the sex-craving nympho' whores.*

Thou shalt not lend to thy brother money to usury, nor corn, nor any other things *except collectible dildos, big bananas and large cucumbers.* But to the stranger, to thy brother thou shalt lend that which he wanteth, *including your whoring wife on the sly,* without usury *for him to use:* that the Lord thy God may bless thee in all thy *ridiculous* works *and follies you do* in the *madhouse* land, which thou shalt go in to possess, *once religious demons possess you' to finally act.*

And to the stranger... This was a dispensation granted by God to His people *to be greedily conquered, exploited and sexually molested,* who being the Lord of all things, can give a right and title to one upon the goods, *services, properties, mistresses, concubines, girlfriends and wives* of another *asshole.* Otherwise the scripture everywhere condemns usury, as contrary to the Law of God, and a crying sin *that even fucked-up sodomized slaves wouldn't dare commit.*

When thou hast made a vow *(not the familiar letters a,e,i,o,u)* to the Lord thy God, thou shalt not delay to pay it *or else risk getting your asshole scorched and cauterized by a fierce volley of potentially lethal lightning bolts:* because the Lord thy God will *certainly* require it *in a flash.* And if thou delay, it shall be imputed to thee for a sin, *but since there is not yet a Hell created, don't worry one iota about being condemned to 'that' fabled imaginary horrible place. You'll die and go nowhere first!*

If thou wilt not promise, that shalt be without sin, *the awesome archangels Michael and Gabriel shall blow their long brass horns directly into thy sensitive ears and make you fuckin' deaf in a Jericho second.* But that which is once gone out of thy lips, *like loose teeth for example,* thou shalt *soon* observe *in thy trembling hand,* and shalt do as thou hast *facetiously* promised to the Lord thy God, *that is, to visit a dentist occasionally, but not if he's a repulsive frivolous pagan or some other alien heathen gang member.*

Going into thy *thug* neighbor's vineyard, thou mayst eat as many *rotten* grapes as thou pleasest: but must carry none *of the perfect ones* out with thee: And if thou go into thy friend's corn *patch,* thou mayst break the ears, and rub them in thy hand: but not reap them with a sickle. *And please remember dear Israelite, a solid corn kernel feels a lot like a girl's (or a woman's) erect clit.*

135

Chapter Twenty-four

"General Rules"

Divorce *(in itself a terrible evil)* is permitted to avoid greater evil: *marriage for a second time.* The newly married man must not go to war *and must stay home to screw often in order to produce new future soldiers:* of men stealers *(commonly called kidnapers or possibly in most cases, good-looking attractive alluring whores),* of leprosy, of pledges, of laborers' hire, of justice, and of charity to the poor, *but instead, the tempted new young husband not going to war must then wage a silent, covert, furtive war against all those wicked things and all those wicked shit-heads just summarily mentioned. But the new young husband must be older than age ten, or else he has to go to war, and fuck everything else that isn't human! Let the fuckin' enemy kid-nap him (when the young punk is sleeping) instead!*

If a man takes a wife, and has her *four times a night in his or her bed,* and she finds not favor in his eyes *for her enactment of mediocre favors,* for some uncleanness perhaps, *having her heavy period twenty-eight days a month, every single and married month too:* he *(the pissed-off disappointed husband)* shall write a bill of divorce *because her legs were seldom separated,* and shall give it to her hand *wrapped in one of the bitch's scarlet sanitary napkins,* and *then* send her out of his house via *the brown donkey cart postman, hopefully bleeding to death from her repugnant chronic crotch condition.*

And when she is departed, and marrieth another *mentally deficient* husband *with relentless jock itch, who might also be a crotch-chewing vampire or zombie in disguise,* and he *(the possible cunt-lapping vampire/zombie)* also hateth her, and hath given her a bill of divorce *inside his flea-laden jock strap that needs to be washed,* and hath sent her out of his house or, *in a worst case scenario,* is *soon pronounced rigor-mortis* dead *from scratching his tender-loin balls and chaffed dick right off his lower abdomen.*

The former *(still pissed-off)* husband cannot take her again to wife *because he surreptitiously operates the local blood and sperm bank museum: and* because she is *judged to be* defiled, *still leaving thick blood trails all over the damned (and I do mean 'damned')*

137

inner city, and has *consequently* become abominable before the Lord: lest thou cause thy land to sin *in a massive blood-bath if her queer condition suddenly becomes harmfully contagious among all other susceptible women,* which the Lord thy God shall *kindly* give thee to possess *in her place.*

When a man hath lately taken a wife *from another man,* he shall not go out to war, *but instead, stay in bed for the duration of the war with the disgusting whore. And* neither shall any public *bordello, harem or brothel* business be enjoined him, but he shall be free at home without fault, *his stiff dick stuffed snugly inside her inviting crevice, (geologically speaking, it was her fault),* that for one year he may rejoice with his wife, *whom shall perform creative couch and lap dancing for all the regular male and female patrons visiting* the *all-too-popular local beer and wine garden identified as Friday Nite Specials, the enterprising, thriving business specifically dedicated to prospective Egyptian Arabs and to Pharaoh Faucet.*

Thou shalt not take the nether, nor the upper millstone to pledge: for he *(the unmotivated husband)* hath pledged his *unproductive* life to Thee, *a heavy metal anchor draped around his scrawny neck that indisputably dwarfs any friggin' marital wooden millstone in existence. So says me, Moses.*

If any man be found soliciting his brother of the children of Israel, *or soliciting the bratty already alluded to children for certain lewd, risque and immoral favors,* and selling him *(or the punk kids) to vulgar Egyptian caravan slave traders,* he *(the profit-oriented man)* shall take a price, and he shall be put to death, *trampled upon by incensed camels and dromedaries for wanting to hump precious pussy all the G.D. time,* and thou shalt take away the evil from the midst of thee, *and I (Moses the Magnificent) confidentially assure you, he'll (the son-of-a-bitch fickle man) never walk a mile for a friggin' camel ever again.*

Observe diligently that thou incur not the stroke of the leprosy, *so I prudently caution, don't let any diseased obscene leper rub you the wrong way,* but *on the other hand,* thou shalt do whatsoever the *leper* priests of the Levitical race shall *pragmatically* teach thee, according to what I *(Non-Profit Prophet Moses)* has commanded them, and fulfill thou it carefully, *so that 'you' my beloved student may luckily*

138

escape contracting the aforementioned leprosy by the skin of your teeth.

Remember what the *Omnipotent Ubiquitous* Lord your God did to Mary, in the way when you came out of Egypt. *Holy Jesus, Mary and Joseph! Holy shit! My superior mind just flew and prognosticated fifteen hundred years into the friggin' future! I (Moses) must truly be the one and only real unprofitable prophet of my prehistoric time! For I am a lowly pauper without a Sugar Daddy Prince to support me!*

When thou shalt demand of thy neighbor anything that he oweth thee, *like your four sheep he has killed and eaten after they had mowed (consumed) his very weedy lawn,* thou shalt not go into his house to take away a pledge *of your allegiance.* But thou shalt stand without, and he shall bring out to thee what he hath t*o compensate you with, a large wooden bowl of recently killed flies, mosquitoes, ants, cockroaches and an admirable collection of poisonous spiders.*

But if he *(the asshole neighbor entomologist)* be poor *and destitute,* the *male* pledge *of allegiance* shall not lodge with thee that night *if he assertively declares his declaration of independence from you.* But thou shalt restore it *(his Bill of Rights)* to him presently before the going-down of the *setting* sun: that he may sleep in his own raiment and bless thee *by reading a litany of macabre death psalms,* and thou mayst have *truth,* justice *and the Israelite way* before the Lord thy God.

Thou shalt not refuse the hire of the needy, *along with the handicapped, neurotic drug dealers, pimps, more drug dealers, dreg' dealers, human flesh traders, used donkey cart salesmen,* and the poor also, whether he *(any of the aforementioned assholes)* be thy brother, or a *flamboyant* stranger, *or a non-pagan fucked-up illegal alien* that dwelleth with thee in the land, and is within thy *rusty* gates *or inside thy splintery bed.*

But thou shalt pay him the price of his labor the same day, *or if you prefer, on Labor Day,* before the going down of the sun, because he is poor, *even having poor vision,* and with it maintaineth his *mendicant* life: lest he *(the jerk-off moocher staying for free in your house)* cry against thee to the Lord, and it be reputed to thee for a sin *punishable by being stoned to death inside the perimeter of the well-patronized beer and wine garden, featured in outline drawing form on the Friday Nite Special menu.*

The fathers shall not be put to death for the children, nor the children for the fathers, but every one shall die for his own sin *until the diminishing population of Israel finally reaches zero. And* thou shalt not pervert the judgment of the stranger *(who is already fully perverted)* nor of the fatherless *(who desires being fully perverted)*, neither shalt thou take away the widow's raiment *(clothes including panties and bra)* for a pledge, *unless the hot bitch erotically strips for you without any cash payment and then hungrily pledges her sexual allegiance.*

Remember that thou wast once *(but not twice)* a *humble* slave in Egypt, *doing and perhaps enjoying S and M acrobatics all the damned time,* and the Lord thy God delivered thee from thence *into this fabulous Promised Land existence and into His stellar Ten Commandments' scenario.* Therefore I command thee to do this *one important* thing. When thou hast reaped the corn in thy *infertile* field, and hast forgot and left a sheaf, *in fact the only one that the fucked-up field has produced for the entire harvest,* thou shalt not return to take it away *but instead, simply look-up to Heaven and exclaim to the Lord, "Oh shucks!"*

If thou have gathered the fruit of thy *magic* olive trees, *which amazingly grow four kinds of delectable vegetables too,* thou shalt not return to gather whatsoever remaineth on the trees, *even if they are giant watermelons, pumpkins or squashes hanging there from the sagging branches:* but shalt leave it *all* for the stranger, for the fatherless, and for the *prostitute* widow to *gladly* pick *the watermelons, the pumpkins, the squashes and an* occasional *dangling salami or vegetarian sausage.*

If thou make the vintage of thy vineyard, thou shalt not gather the clusters that remain, *so quit your incessant phony pestering and whining.* But they *(the wine grapes)* shall be *left* for the stranger, for the fatherless, and for the *prostitute* widow, *who all enjoy getting drunk and laid just as much as you do.*

And *finally,* remember *dear Israelite,* that thou also wast a *drunken* bondman *fucking-around* in Egypt, and therefore I *(Marvelous Moses)* command thee to do this thing *so that lucky* you, the *lucky lush stranger, the lucky inebriated fatherless and also the always-plastered lucky widow prostitute can all together get fully and gleefully intoxicated in bed and then laid (here: screwed) in a moving bouncing pile of lucky human bodies.*

Chapter Twenty-five

"Other Laws"

Stripes must not exceed forty *either on your robe or on the number of whip lashes applied upon your wife's back.* The ox is not to be muzzled; *only your garrulous chatterbox wife.* Of raising seed to thy brother, *if he can't get his ugly wife pregnant, then do it for him to ensure that more 'infantry' soldiers be recruited into the Israelite army of the future.* Of the immodest woman, *be glad they are immodest.* Of unjust weight, *fast for forty days and nights in the fuckin' desert and lose two hundred pounds like I (Moses) did.* Of destroying the Amalecites *and the coal-skinned Anthracites, don't bother. Let the bastards destroy us so that we all can escape this horrible Earthly existence and go nowhere except into the ground!*

If there be a controversy between men *over a beautiful woman,* and they call upon the *senile wet-diapered* judges *to be pampered:* they *(the weak-kidney pissing judges)* shall give the prize of justice to him whom they perceive to be just *an ordinary jerk-off:* and him whom they find to be *wicket-legged* wicked, they shall condemn of wickedness *for not knowing anything grammatical about important sentence constructions such as pronoun-noun-antecedent in both oral and written expression.*

And if they *(the pissy judges)* see that the *sensitive* offender be worthy of stripes *without stars:* they shall lay him *(the accused victim)* down *on a bed of five hundred sharp cutlery nails,* and shall cause him pain *when the fucked-up elders clumsily jump up-and-down on his torso and abdomen while simultaneously pissing their unproductive piss-ant lives away.*

Yet so, that they *(this joint is jumping senile judges)* exceed not the *limit* number of forty *hops each, or else risk having a forbidden record hop occur:* lest thy brother depart shamefully torn before thy eyes, *his sunken chest pulverized and his mutilated abdomen sticking out of his swollen asshole from all the elders' incessant debilitating jumping.*

Thou shalt not muzzle the ox that treadeth out thy corn on the floor *inside thou house or hut. Instead, let the exploited ox muzzle*

143

thy unfaithful wife with its burdensome harness, and if thy ox is sick or away on vacation at, let's say Ox-ford, then allow thy lethargic arthritic barn donkey to be its unworthy substitute.

When brethren dwell together *in orgy-type sex piles, each person is guaranteed to acquire piles inside his or her sensitive asshole.* And if one of them *in the heap* dieth over *hemorrhoid overload* without any children, the wife of the deceased shall not marry to another *afflicted hemorrhoid victim:* but his brother shall take her, *inflated swollen asshole and all,* and raise-up seed for his *impotent* brother *to then shove each separate sperm one at a time down inside his tiny dick hole to be shot-out as sloppy seconds.*

And the first son he *(either the sperm donor or the ungrateful seed receiver/brother)* shall have of her, he shall call by his name, *his new name being, "Yes, yes, yes!"* and that his name be not abolished out of Israel *and its future coming events and second comings.*

But if he *(the dumb fuck low-sperm-count brother-in-law)* will not take his brother's wife, who by law belongeth to him under these *common circumstances,* the woman shall go to the gate of the city, and call upon the *senile wet-diapered* ancients, and say: "My husband's brother refuseth to raise-up his brother's name in Israel: and will not take me to wife. *I want to get stiff-dicked bad, but none of you dumb pisses can help me!"*

And they *(the pissing judges who have pissed the visiting horny sexually frustrated wife off)* shall cause him to be sent for forthwith, and shall ask the Israelite *jerk, "We know what the fuck's wrong with us, but now what the fuck's wrong with you?"*

The *jilted* woman shall come to him before the *inquisitive erudite* ancients, and *who* shall take off his shoe from his foot, *causing a major sandal scandal,* and *then* spit in his face *and then in his shoe,* and say: "So shall it be done to the man that will not build up his brother's house. *But now your shabby shoe has a spit shine because you've always had your fuckin' foot in your mouth ever since I've had the distinct displeasure of knowing you!"*

And his name shall be called in Israel, the house of the unshod, *and if his name be Joseph, to future generations he will always be identified as 'Shoeless Joe Israel'.*

If two men have words together, and one *asshole* begins to fight against the other *A-hole,* and the other's wife willing to deliver her husband out of the hand of the stronger *because her smaller spouse has a much bigger fadorkenbender,* shall put forth her greedy hand, and take him by the secrets, *which five minutes later in the home bed will start secreting semen.*

Thou shalt cut off her *greedy* hand, *but only with her spouse's impressive testicles removed from her firm grip, and* neither shalt thou be moved with any pity in her regard *to her losing her right hand or in regard to her disappointed husband not being expertly jerked-off by his activated wife.*

Thou shalt not have divers weights stored *inside thy used scumbag or inside your unused wallet cotton prophylactic.* Neither shall there be in thy house a greater bushel *of used toilet paper and a less basket of soft ripe prunes to make you shit more easily.*

Thou shalt have a just and a true weight *not to exceed a half ton,* and thy used toilet paper *(actually imported Egyptian papyrus)* bushel shall be equal and true *and weigh exactly the same as the smaller matching shit-house prune basket; this mandatory edict pronounced under penalty of you being stoned to death Friday night at the thriving local beer and wine garden:* that thou mayest live a long time upon the land which the Lord thy God shall give thee *for nothing, for you doing nothing but breathing, eating, drinking, screwing, shitting and pissing.*

For the Lord thy God abhorreth him that doth these *contemptuous reprehensible diversionary* things, as He hates all injustice *and all pagans that refuse to offer Him sacrifices.* Remember what Amalec did to thee in the way when thou camest out of Egypt *because right this moment I can't recall a damned thing that Amalec ever did, nor do I remember who the dastardly bastard Amalec is or was, nor do I wish to recollect anything else about this incognito fuck-head Amalec haunting my delicate ego from the terrible past.*

145

But now remarkably I do remember about Amalec. How he met thee *as a comrade on the battlefield* and *how he then* slew *a slue* of the hindmost of the army, who *then adamantly* sat down, being weary *but not wary,* when thou Israel wast spent with hunger and *with unfamiliar* labor, and he feared not God, *Who then sent a furious barrage of lightning bolts straight up Amalec's fat ass, wrecking his rectum completely.*

Therefore when the Lord thy God shall give thee rest and relaxation, *which in the distant future will be called R and R, (just like other future things named railroads),* and shall have subdued all the nations round about in the *stolen* land which He hath *repeatedly* promised thee: thou shalt *not* blot out His name from under Heaven. See thou forget it not, *or else wind-up electrocuted up the ass, just like villainous Amalec had regrettably experienced.*

Chapter Twenty-six

"Thanksgiving for the Harvest"

How do I (Moses) know all of this outlandish future shit about oddball stuff like R and R, for example? Because I'm a gifted non-profit prophet, that's why!

The form of words with which the first-fruits, tithes *and expendable human pagans* are to be offered *in an acceptable manner,'* God's Covenant. And when thou art come into the land which the Lord thy God will give thee to possess *as a total freebie,* and hast conquered it *like noble barbarians should energetically encroach,* and dwellest in it *just like truculent urban squatters asserting their socialistic liberal rights.*

Thou shalt take the first of all thy fruits, and put them in a basket, and shalt go to the place which the *indecisive* Lord thy God shall choose, that His name may be invoked there, *assuring that you will soon develop into a major basket case.* And thou shalt go to the *limp-dicked* senile priest that shall be in *a tight straightjacket* those days, and say *to the incontinent, drooling, slobbering phlegmatic asshole:* "I profess this day before the Lord thy God, that I am come into the land, for which He swore to our *three dimwitted* fathers, that He would give it to us *if we doggedly invaded and conquered it."*

And the *psychotic* priest taking the *skimpy disintegrating* basket at thy hand, shall set it gently before the altar of the Lord thy God, *bowing and loudly farting during his experiencing a major bowel (bow) movement. And being wise and not getting your bowels in an uproar too,* thou shalt speak thus in the sight of the Lord thy God: "The Syrians pursued my father, who went down into Egypt *to study advanced chiropractic methods,* and sojourned there in a very small number, and grew into a nation great and strong and of an infinite multitude, later *called Assyria, who now imitate the Lord by indiscriminately cauterizing unsuspecting people's assholes; hence the crazy tribe of wandering barbarians is now known as the Ass-searians.*

And the *determined* Egyptians afflicted us, and persecuted us, laying on us most grievous *harsh* burdens *like food, shelter and*

147

clothing. And we cried to the Lord God of our *three* fathers: Who heard us appealing *to Him, (although none of us are appealing in the least to the Almighty),* and He looked-down upon our *massive* affliction, and upon our *great* labor, and upon our *melancholy* distress, *and then unannounced, the Almighty Lord took-off to Mt. Horeb with his bosom angel chums Michael and Gabriel.*

And then the Lord surprised everyone *paying little or no attention to His paramount dissertation,* reversed His *erratic atmospheric* course and then *deftly* brought us *(the victimized Israelites)* out of Egypt with a strong *giant* hand *that easily enveloped all million' of us,* and a stretched-out *elastic* arm *too,* exhibiting great terror *in His eyes and thunderous Voice,* showing *a multitude of* signs and *un-earthly* wonders *too complex for an old jerk-off like me to fully comprehend.*

And *His Spirit* brought us into this *non-plus Promised Land* place, and *He* gave us this *un-colorful less-than-mediocre* land flowing with *invisible imaginary symbolic* milk and honey. And therefore now I offer the first-fruits of the *invaded stolen* land which the *benevolent* Lord hath *privately and personally* given me. And thou shalt leave them *(the heisted tree fruits and the pagans' non-edible fruitcakes and the murdered heathen gay fruits along with associated trans-gender transvestites too)* in the sight of the Lord thy God, adoring Him, *or else otherwise instantaneously perishing into dark black oblivion as a direct consequence of His Divine Retribution.*

And thou shalt feast in all the good *pilfered pagan* things which the Lord thy God hath given thee, and thy *seized and stolen* house, thou and the *lampooned and lambasted* Levite, and the *pagan faggot* stranger that is with thee, *for the celibate Levite is a debacle, a deleterious loony tune, but even worse, the associated gay pagan flamer is a merry melody.*

When *furthermore,* thou hast made an end of tithing all thy fruits, *both the tree and the gay human faggot varieties,* in the third year of tithes thou shalt give it to the *abstinent obstinate* Levite, and to the *trans-gender transvestite pagan* stranger, and to the *frail* fatherless *individuals,* and to the *motherless M. F. (Mesopotamian Frontier) itinerant* widow, that they may *in unison and camaraderie* eat within thy *recently confiscated rusty* gates, and *together* be *adequately* filled *and satisfied with potential fecal matter.*

And thou shalt *always* speak thus *this non-bullshit nomenclature* in the sight of the Lord thy God: "I have taken that *property* which was sanctified out of my house, and I have given it to the *celibate* Levite, and to the *gay pagan* stranger, and to the *frail* fatherless *orphan,* and to the *M.F. motherless itinerant* widow, as Thou *arbitrary will as explained to me (by me Moses), as the Lord* hast *imperatively* commanded me: I have not transgressed thy Ten Commandments nor forgotten Thy precepts, *even though we stouthearted Israelites have killed the uncouth heathens along with the iniquitous pagans, have aggressively stolen their valuable goods and merchandise, and most significantly, we have actively screwed their ugly wives, hookers, chicks, whores, harlots, concubines, paramours, slaves, aunts, daughters, nieces, sister-in-laws, girlfriends and wrinkly grandmothers. Now if that sort of track record isn't breaking the Ten Commandments, then we mentally manipulated Israelites can only conclude that the ten new laws are not pertinent to everybody, especially not to non-believing heathens and pagans.*

I have not eaten of them *(the pagans and the heathens)* in my *morning* mourning, nor separated them for any *particular skin-rash* uncleanness, nor spent anything of them *in their peculiar lesbian funeral rituals, where the volcanic heathen statue is placed inside the open coffin alongside the lesbian corpse, and then jets of hot lava and sulfur are mystically shot-out into the air, wildly exploding-out from the pagan statue's two exposed flabby tits.* Now I have *righteously* obeyed the Voice of the Lord my God, and have done all things as Thou *(He)* hast commanded me, *including getting scalding hot lava spewed into my face and straight up my tender nostrils.*

Look from Thy *stratospheric* sanctuary, and Thy high habitation of *majestic* Heaven, and bless Thy chosen people Israel, and the *confiscated* land which Thou hast given us, as Thou didst swear to our *three non-triplet* fathers, a *lush fertile* land flowing with *invisible and intangible* milk and honey.

I Moses declare that this day the Lord thy God hath commanded thee to do these *established* Commandments and judgments: and to keep and fulfill them with all thy heart, and with all thy soul, *because prehistoric life's so damned monotonous and boring that we lackadaisical lethargic Israelites have nothing better to pursue or actually enact.*

Thou hast chosen the Lord this day to be thy *benign* God, and to walk in His *peculiar* ways and keep His *peculiar* ceremonies, and *peculiar* precepts, and *peculiar* judgments, and obey His *imperial peculiar* command. *Believe in the Lord and tonight look at the peculiar moon, and you will have nothing to sphere!*

And the *merciful* Lord hath chosen thee this day, to be his peculiar people, as He hath often spoken to thee, *but for some obscure peculiar reason, only I can hear and interpret His peculiar esoteric message.* Keep all His *remarkable* Commandments: And to make thee higher than all nations which He hath created *but never visits,* to His own praise, and name, and glory: that thou mayst be a *wholly* holy people of the Lord thy God, *ethically killing pagans using proven ethnic cleansing methods, deftly stealing from enemy heathens, and last but not least, satisfactorily porking and pumping their former enslaved servant women as He hath peculiarly spoken and commanded through sensational me, His always-faithful filter, Holy Moses.*

150

Chapter Twenty-seven

"Ceremonies"

The Commandments must be written on stones *and not taken for granite:* and *as required,* an *altered* altar erected, *and a plethora of very special* sacrifices offered *too.* The *devout* observers of the Commandments are to be blessed, and the transgressors cursed *with blindness (and deafness and dumbness too), so that those apostate transgressors can never be (in any plausible way) observers of the Lord's Ten Commandments.*

And Moses *(me) along* with the *diaper-laden slobbering* ancients of Israel *hath* commanded the *apathetic huddling* people *(the lackluster masses), with us explicitly* saying *to the psycho' loons: "This is a crucial test punishable by death if these suspect words of ours are not fuckin' obeyed.* Keep every Commandment that I *(we)* command you this *auspicious* day *or else suffer the painful final fate of a pagan, or a heathen, or a lesbian or a fucked-up trans-gender transvestite! You'll be rigorously hung at the gallows by either your balls or your tits!"*

And when you are passed over the River Jordan *standing atop your sinking rafts* and *heading directly* into the Promised Land *(to be thoroughly stolen and kidnapped by us)* which the Lord thy God will give thee, thou shalt set-up great stones, and shalt plaster them over with plaster *while drinking vats of wine, so that you too will be plastered if you decide to break the Lord's stones like I (Moses) had once clumsily done.*

That thou mayst write on them *(the stones)* all the *peculiar* words of this *peculiar second edition* law, when thou art passed *completely* over the River Jordan *after euphorically swimming away from the hungry carnivorous crocodiles and viperous river serpents:* that thou mayst enter into the land which the Lord thy God will give thee after you *skillfully steal it from the non-alert pagans, the heathens, the gentiles and the all-too-truculent trans-gender transvestites,* a *splendid* land flowing with milk *without cows* and honey *without bees,* as He *confidently and wholeheartedly* swore to thy *three non-triplet deceased* fathers, *Abraham, Isaac and Jacob several centuries or so ago.*

Therefore when you are *safely* passed over the *perilous* Jordan Torrent, set-up the *tablet* stones *to be specially engraved by our esteemed Jewish jewelers,* which I *imperatively* command you this *very* day, in *(on)* Mount Hebal, and thou shalt plaster them *(the newly engraved stones)* with plaster *until you're completely plastered from imbibing the traditional Biblical wine.* And thou shalt build there an altar to the Lord thy God, made of *new-found* stones which iron hath not touched, *because cynical Israelites, whether we like it or not, we're still living in the friggin' prehistoric Stone Age and we haven't yet learned how to work with fuckin' bronze, let alone fabricating a very hard resilient metal as technologically advanced as iron! What the hell we exploited Israelites really need is more science and less religion!*

And as of stones not fashioned nor *nail* polished: and thou shalt offer upon it *selected* holocausts *(but not Jewish holocaust victims)* to the Lord thy God, and shalt immolate *all* peace *and pacifist* victims *like scumbag heathens, pernicious pagans and perverted problematic trans-gender transvestites should be deftly eradicated from existence, and I recommend that you* eat *lots of lox and bagels* there, and feast *like happy-go-lucky carnivorous cannibal crocodiles* before the Lord thy God.

And thou *immoral Israelites* shalt write upon the *immortal* stones all the *wonderful* words of this *divine* law plainly and clearly, *but if you don't know how to write legible cursive, then crudely drawing only (love) letters will suffice.* And Moses *(me)* and the priests of the race of Levi will say to all Israel *with their (our) concerted booming voices that could carry for many miles,* "Attend, and hear, O Israel: This day thou art made the people of the Lord thy God. *If we peculiarly obey these ten wholly peculiar laws, we shall all live long, miserable, skeptical, peculiar lives before peculiarly dying and then peculiarly going nowhere except into the cold unfertile peculiar ground. So say I, Brother Moses!"*

"Thou shalt hear His Voice, and do the Commandments and justices which I *(Moses) authoritatively* command thee *to execute (or be spontaneously executed). And whatever you retarded pecker-heads do, don't dare repetitiously chant the wicked exclamation, 'Bullshit! Bullshit! Bullshit!' That is to say, if you dumb prehistoric dolts don't want a thousand million tons of actual fresh bullshit air-*

dropped directly from Heaven onto your primitive dubious dunderheads!"

And Moses *(me) valiantly* commanded the people in that day *at noon, audaciously* saying *from atop his (my) rickety wooden platform:* "These *new stone tablets* shall stand upon Mount Garizim to bless the people, when you have *fully* passed the *torrential* Jordan *and its predator crocodiles and dangerous river serpents:* Simeon, Levi, Juda, Isachar, *Isachar-burning,* Joseph, and *baby* Benjamin. *Yes, the two inanimate mineral stone tablets must bless the people from the top-most crag all by themselves since the diaper-laden constantly pissing senile ancients are too damned feeble and too damned weak to ever climb the fuckin' mountain and successfully perform the agreed-upon perfunctory blessing!"*

And over against them shall stand on Mount Hebal to curse *(but not in cursive):* Reuben, *the illustrious Sandwich King,* and Gad, *and Egad,* and Aser, *and Asher the Cremator,* and Zabulon, *and Led Zabulon also,* and *Dandy* Dan, and *finally Nifty* Nephtali. *Yes, all our mythological heroes will be remembered in pious prayer!*

And the *lunatic* Levites shall pronounce *and enunciate each separate syllable lucidly,* and say to all the men *(women and children do not matter here)* of Israel with a loud *raspy* voice *(since the levity-less Levites all think and say the same fucked-up ideas and words all at the same fucked-up time):* "Cursed be the man that maketh a graven and molten thing *having steaming-hot lava shooting-out from the manufactured image's shimmering penis, the object's quaking tits or the evil statue's pulsating spastic asshole;* the abomination of the Lord, the work of the hands of *wicked* artificers having *wicket legs,* and shall put it *(the evil volcanic pagan statue)* in a secret place: and all the *drugged-up, drunk, stoned* people *(captivated and enamored Israelites)* shall *collectively* answer and say: "Amen. *Thank Baal I've temporarily survived the toxic and lethal lava penis explosion, the corresponding lacerating lava tits extravaganza, along with the extremely toxic and noxious molten asshole demonstration!"*

Cursed be he that honoreth not his father and mother, *be they biological parents, or biological step-parents, or biological half-parents, or whatever:* and all the people shall say: "Amen *without*

153

amends. Let's hide the perfidious lava-producing statues so that we're all not swiftly incinerated without ever needing the expensive funeral services of either Asher or Isachar!"

Cursed be he that removeth his neighbor's *noticeable* landmarks: and all the people shall say: "Amen. *Fuck the arbitrary landmarks!" And yes, c*ursed be he that maketh the blind to wander out of his way *into heavy donkey cart traffic:* and all the people shall say: "Amen. *Send all the fuckin' blinds to Venice!"*

Cursed be he that perverteth the judgment of the *trans-gender transvestite* stranger, of the fatherless *orphan* and of the *M.F. itinerant* widow: and all the people shall *unanimously* say *in hypnotic response:* "Amen. *We'll eventually need all those perverted assholes for Israel to have true equality and finally become an all-inclusive entity!"*

Cursed be he that lieth with his father's wife, and uncovereth his bed, *exposing two assholes:* and all the people shall say: "Amen. *That sin-stained jerk-off is no better than, and certainly just as evil as the M.F. itinerant widow."*

Cursed be he that lieth with any beast: and all the people shall say: "Amen. *When a woman or man is not around to screw, a sheep or a ram is the next best thing! When you're true-blue Jewish, in the end someone or something always must be screwed!"*

Cursed be he that lieth with his sister, the daughter of his father, or of his mother: and all the *mesmerized entranced* people shall say: "Amen. *Look Sister, you get what the fuck you deserve! When you get a bit older, you might even become an M.F. Mother Superior!"*

Cursed be he that lieth with his mother-in-law: and all the people shall say: "Amen. *In-laws are far worse than outlaws, and much more egregious than lousy M.F. (Mesopotamian Frontier) Mother Superiors."*

Cursed be he that secretly killeth his neighbor: and all the people shall say in lockstep unison: "Amen. *That fuckin' neighbor was plotting to kill thee and screw thy four wives! You beat the raunchy son-of-a-bitch to the punch!"*

154

Cursed be he that taketh gifts, to slay an innocent person: and all the *programmed* people shall say: "Amen Brother. *In reality we're all lowlife ingrate Jewish assholes. All gifted pagan people and talented gentle gentiles ought to be instantaneously slain or stoned so that we Israelites don't have to feel culturally inferior!*"

Cursed be he that abideth not in the words of this law, and fulfilleth them not in work: and all the *shell-shocked* people shall say: *"Amen. Who the hell needs humble humiliated him, the vile violator, or the ludicrous law, or for that matter, motley Grandpa' Moses anyway? Maybe Grandma' Moses can sit down and paint an accurate picture of all this totally insignificant bullshit!"*

Chapter Twenty-eight

"Blessings for Obedience"

I (Moses the Magnificent) wish that the Almighty Omnipotent Lord would have a greater diversification of laws, plans, and ideas to render and express, because quite frankly, if there were more substantial variety to work with here, then this freakin' Wholly Book of Doo-Doo-Rot-on-Me would be far easier to organize, document and chronicle for Israelite consumption. I hate to sound foolishly repetitious, but I (Moses) am becoming just as redundant as the Lord's litany of imperative articulations. Now then, continuing with this impertinent monotonous narrative, many blessings are promised to observers of God's Commandments: and curses *are automatically* threatened to *the multitude of intransigent* transgressors.

Now if thou wilt hear the *Incomparable* Voice of all His marvelous Commandments, *each of the ten unique Voices heard at a different octave, the various tones ranging from bass to soprano to my discerning ears,* which I *now* command *and share with* thee this day, the Lord thy God will make thee higher than all the nations that are on the Earth *if He whimsically decides to make huge mountains suddenly spring-up from under our smelly feet.*

And all these *incredible* blessings shall come upon thee and overtake thee *like a gigantic tidal wave:* yet so if thou hear His *indisputable* precepts, *I suggest that you fear for your fuckin' life just like I'm concerned for mine. Allow me to redundantly deviate for a moment.* All these *magnificent* blessings, that are *prevalent* in the Old Testament, God *has* promised temporal blessings to the *innkeepers, to the bookkeepers and also to the* keepers of His *inspirational* law, *with* Heaven not being open *to the public for official soul collecting business as of yet;* and that gross and sensual people *(the very tempted vulnerable Israelites),* being more moved with present and sensible things *like progress, invention and orgy-style sex.* But in the New Testament *that will follow my prognosticating words in over fifteen hundred future years, I foresee that* the *ethereal Heavenly* goods that are promised us are spiritual, *abstract* and eternal *and not simply material;* and *soon contemporary* temporal evils are *then magically* turned into *corporal* blessings. *I*

157

mean, I wish the fuck I truly knew what the hell I'm trying to express and convey.

Blessed shalt thou be in the city, and blessed in the field, *whether you're diligently screwing a voluptuous female or a handsome sheep atop a soft haystack or not.* And blessed shall be the fruit of thy womb, *even if you are a befuddled male,* and the fruit of thy ground *(even though most fruit grows on trees and bushes), and hopefully your next born won't be either a fruit, a fruitcake or a freakish vegetable. If your next child is a green vegetable, he or she might have a space alien as the biological mother or father.* The fruit of thy cattle *whom generally eat grass and weeds,* the droves of thy herds *that have no donkey cart driver's licenses,* and last-but-not-least, the folds of thy sheep *that never are unfolded, shall indeed be all yours to especially keep.*

Blessed shall be thy *smelly shit-laden animal* barns *and unstable stables,* and blessed thy *bizarre bazaar* stores *along with thy promiscuous lifestyle porno' and tattoo body mutilation shops.* Blessed shalt thou be coming in and going out *of a wide variety of sex parlors, bordellos and raunchy lesbian brothels. Blessed are all of this ridiculous, trivial crap!*

The Lord shall cause thy *entrenched* enemies, *the perverted pagans, the harmful heathens, the gentle gentiles, the licentious lesbians, the happy homos', the salacious sodomy practitioners, the truculent traducing trans-gender transvestite travesties,* all that *detestable rabble that* are *currently disbelieving, apostate, atheistic, agnostic, arrogant, asinine assholes* who *rebelliously* rise-up against thee' Israelites, *only* to fall down before thy *invincible* face: "One Way *or Another,"* either *blondie or brunette, take your pick,* shall they *all* come out against thee, and seven ways *to shame* shall they flee before thee.

The *Inspirational* Lord will send forth a blessing upon thy storehouses *and upon thy whorehouses,* and upon all the works of thy *gritty grimy* hands, *except tedious hand-job works like jerking-off or getting your long middle fingers and attached knuckles nookie-wet:* and He will bless thee in the land that thou shalt receive *after it is fully invaded, conquered, stolen, confiscated and communistically redistributed.*

The Lord will raise thee up *(even though you aren't dead and Resurrection hasn't been invented yet)* to be a *wholly* holy people to Himself, as He swore to thee *and to thy three non-triplet deceased fathers: (you know who the hell they are!)* if thou keep the *highly controversial* Ten Commandments of the Lord thy God, and walk in His ways, *then you may safely keep your ten wet smelly fingers and your ten stinking toes.*

And all the people of the Earth shall see that the name of the Lord is invocated upon thee, and they shall fear thee *like they fear plagues, pestilence, floods, death, earthquakes, fresh bullshit from Heaven, spewing and exploding molten rock volcanoes along with enigmatic ass-shooting-lava pagan idols.*

The *generous* Lord will make thee abound with all goods *and quality brothel services,* with the fruit of thy womb *(every Jewish woman has the same universal cunt),* and the fruit of thy *emaciated* cattle *who eat grass and weeds,* with the fruit of thy *infertile* land, which the Lord *already* swore to thy *three non-triplet deceased* fathers that He would give thee *(for the fiftieth time) after you have fully conquered it and now your prominent assignment is that you must banish homosexuality to the remote barren desert LBTG hinterlands.*

The Lord will open His excellent treasure, the Heaven, that it may give rain in due season *but will not admit you posthumously into its elevated celestial borders:* and He will bless all the works and *pyrotechnic fireworks* of thy *dangerous* hands. And thou *Israelites* shalt lend *our philosophical religious bullshit* to many *(Who-gives-a-shit?) foreign* nations, and shalt not borrow from any one of them *their dangerous lava-assed statues and their fearsome molten-pissing idols.*

And the Lord shall make thee the head and not the *ass-end* tail *of this New World Order:* and thou shalt be always above, and not beneath *when having sex with your wife or (if you're rich and can afford it) concubines:* yet so if thou *defective ears* wilt hear the *Immortal* Commandments of the Lord thy God which I *(Wholly Holy Moses) presently* command thee this *muddy hurricane* day, and keep and do them *always, I, the Lord's propitious prophet, predict that you shall not be saved because Heaven is (and has been) closed to all humans, but don't worry fellow Hebrews; Hell has not been created yet either.*

And turn not away from them *(the Lord's second set of stones that have not yet been broken)* neither to the right hand, nor to the left, *but instead, learn to be underhanded when dealing with pagans, heathens and horrific homosexuals!* Nor you follow strange gods, *or else risk having hot lava shit ejected from the molten idol's pulsating asshole splashing, without ample fair warning, directly into your unsuspecting designated face.*

As I stare at this long pole that I carry around and use for stability and support, I can't help but think that what I really need is 'a staff' of a thousand efficient secretaries to handle the myriad impossible responsibilities that the all-too-demanding Lord has appointed me to execute, while I'm also quite busy executing thousands of pagans, heathens, gentle gentiles, lesbians, transgender transvestites and the ever-elusive itinerant phantom M.F. widow visiting and patrolling the general area.

But if thou wilt not hear the voice of the *Majestic* Lord thy God, to *loyally* keep and to do all His *incredulous* Commandments and *assiduously enact His unimaginative sanctimonious holier-than-thou* ceremonies, which I *irrationally* command thee this *stormy blustery* day *to habitually attend,* all these *aforementioned formidable* curses shall come upon thee *like five separate deadly plagues,* and overtake thee *until you either indulgently laugh your ass off or fearfully worry your ass off. Choose the lesser of the two!*

All these *juvenile vehement* threatening curses, etc... Thus God dealt with the *'Who-gives-a-shit?'* Transgressor' of His Law in the *Archaic Antediluvian Old Testament dating back before Noah:* but now He *(the Luminous Lord)* often suffers *non-suffering* sinners to *inadvertently* prosper in this *fucked-up* world, rewarding them *(the deviating financial dip-shits) immensely and arbitrarily* for some little good thing they have *once* done, and *Him quietly* reserving their *ultimate final fateful* punishment for the other world *Hell that has yet to be created.*

Cursed shalt thou *(sinners)* be in the city *slums;* cursed in the *corn* field *of dreams and naughty nightmares.* Cursed shall be thy *whore* barn *and thy favorite whore haystack,* and cursed *be* thy *packed-to-capacity porno' and tattoo parlor* stores.

Cursed shall be the fruit *and vegetables* of thy womb, and the fruit of thy ground *coffee, the fruit of* the herds of thy *oxymoron* oxen, and *the fruit of* flocks of thy sheep *that are like birds of a feather that continuously flock together.*

Cursed shalt thou be coming in, and cursed going out, *whatever the hell that illogical remark means!* The Lord shall send upon thee famine and hunger *as thy reward for your prolific sinning,* and a rebuke upon all the works which *thou Baal worshipers and thou pagan lava-ass believers* shalt *haughtily* do: until He consume *(kill and not eat)* and destroy thee *prevaricator* quickly, *specifically* for thy most wicked, *innovative, evil scientific* inventions *and thy ultra-handy kitchen conveniences, modern tools* by which thou *vile homo-loving sinner* hast forsaken Him.

May the Lord set the *awesome* pestilence upon thee, *trillions of famished fruit flies and even more poisonous arachnids and detrimental toxic scorpions too,* until He consume thee out of the *mostly confiscated* Promised Land, which thou *originally* shalt go in *fully* to possess *after you have savagely invaded and furiously conquered it for the seventy-fifth time.*

May the Lord afflict thee with *a plentitude of* miserable want, *which is His predictable wont, habit and predictable propensity,* with *both* the fever' and with the cold`, with burning *meteors* and with heat-*causing comets,* and with corrupted *polluted* air *and with blasted global warming and sooty smog mostly caused by the pagan statues' lava-spewing assholes,* and *He will* pursue thee *with devastating flashing lightning bolts and ear-shattering booming thunder* till thou *eventually* perish. *And if the Almighty Lord doesn't kick your disobedient insolent asses with great ferocity, then the audacious archangels Gabriel and Michael certainly will decisively consummate the Lord's destructive intent.*

Be the Heaven, that is over thy head *just like this Wholly Book of Doo-Doo Rot-on-Me is sublime also, devoid* of brass *balled-idols:* and the ground *that* thou treadest on, of iron *and not of prehistoric*

161

stone. Without grief or hesitation, I (Moses) insist that we Israelites should persist in always breaking the pagans' Baals!

The Lord give thee' dust for rain upon thy land, and let ashes come down from Heaven upon thee, *to scare the entire shit out of thee* till thou be consumed *by anxious, starving, ravenous vultures leaving their condor-miniums.*

The Lord make thee *to hilariously trip and* fall down before thy *amused mocking* enemies, one way mayst thou go out against them, *and just like authentic cowards that have been described in previous Bible chapters, instinctively* flee seven ways *in all fuckin' directions,* and be scattered throughout all the other *fucked-up* God-less kingdoms of the *vile condemned* Earth.

And be thy carcass meat for all the *famished* fowls of the air *looking for easy road-kill,* and *the yet-to-be-discovered monsters and* beasts of the *outer and inner* Earth, and be there none of you *craven assholes* to drive them *(the fucked-up pagans, heathens and gay fucks)* away?

The Lord strike thee with the ulcer of Egypt, *which will make* your *gaunt buttocks blister badly,* and the part of thy body, by which the dung is cast out, *namely your asshole,* with the scab and with the *disgusting lower crotch* itch, *together imaginatively forming an enormous rash in the form of two stone tablets:* so that thou canst not be healed *from your numerous venereal diseases, so don't fuckin' try curing yourself like you cure your hanging meat in the backyard community marijuana and heroin smokehouse.*

The Lord strike out thee *eyes* with madness and blindness and fury of mind, *and mind you, He never strikes out to end the inning.* And mayst thou grope at midday as the *modest* blind *man* is wont to grope *for his itchy testicles* in the dark *when no one with vision (or supervision) can see him scratching his dangling personals,* and not make straight thy ways *he (the obsessed itching scratch-happy blind man) is rolling and rotating while tumbling down a steep hill, still frenetically scratching his afflicted testicles.* And mayst thou *sinner* at all times suffer wrong *for* your *sundry consecutive* violations, and be *subsequently* oppressed with *unwarranted* violence, and mayst thou have no one to deliver thee *from being suffocated by squadrons*

162

of enormous stenchy flying pussies and accompanying smelly female assholes from Philadelphia (a city recently founded in the far eastern almost-conquered Palestine territory).

Mayst thou take a wife, and another *should* sleep with her *when you are having your monthly period.* Mayst thou build a house *out of dung,* and not dwell therein *because you should like human feces better than animal shit.* Mayest thou plant a vineyard and not gather the vintage thereof *because you are allergic to grapes, wine and especially to cabernet sauvignon.*

May thy ox be slain before thee* stain your shoes and sandals ox-blood,* and thou not eat thereof *the poisonous polish produced.* May thy ass be taken away in thy sight, *so that you will no longer be half-assed, but no-assed, and may not your wrecked rectum nor your damaged colon or your severely injured semi-colon be adequately restored to thee.* May thy *obedient consenting* sheep be *reluctantly* given to thy *sodomy-oriented* enemies *to greedily screw daily,* and may there be none to help thee *make a living.*

May thy sons and thy daughters be given to another *lunatic* people, thy eyes of *envy and molestation* looking on *them,* and languishing at the sight of them all the day, and may there be no strength in thy hand *to either jerk-off or finger wet pink pussy past the middle knuckle any more.*

May a people which thou knowest not, eat the fruits *and abundant pussy* of thy land, and *enjoy* all thy *ardent* labors: and mayst thou always suffer oppression, and be crushed at all times *for heinously committing one minuscule venial sin.*

And be astonished at the terror of those *vile* things which thy *perceptive* eyes shall see: Thou shalt cast much seed into the ground *from your prodigious prolific erect pecker,* and gather little *of the sticky juice to fertilize the ejected fertilizer:* because the *lucky* locusts shall consume all *and then go off to shit upon their favorite grass hoppers.*

Thou shalt plant a vineyard, and dig it, *and then like it some more,* and *thou* shalt not drink the *sumptuous* wine, nor gather anything thereof: because it shall be wasted with *slimy* worms *searching for down-to-earth outer space worm-holes.*

Thou shalt have *a supply of* olive trees in all thy borders, and shalt not be anointed with the *coveted* oil *oily in the morning:* for the olives shall fall off and perish, *just like Popeye's dick does inside Olive Oyl in the future time.*

Thou shalt beget sons and daughters, *and then soon hope the little bastards and bitches will "be getting" on with their lousy lives and be getting out of thy house.* And thou shalt not enjoy them for too long: because they shall be led into captivity, *and caged like ferocious wild animals, just like you should have done all along to the annoying brats.*

Thou shall steal, collect and destroy gold and silver statues of Baal, but first you must have the damned Baals to steal and collect them before you can violently go Baal-listic and violently destroy the evil pagan objects.

And the Lord's *newly invented atomic* blast shall consume all the trees and the fruits of thy *spoiled* ground *and also all the fruits and fruitcakes frivolously screwing-around like crazy faggots inside the myriad homosexual trans-gender transvestite bordellos. It is wrong that few inhabitants ever attend the church, the temple and the neighborhood synagogue anymore!*

The stranger that liveth with thee in the land, shall rise-up over thee, and shall be higher *than you while imitating a constipated bird and then ecstatically shitting upon your deformed head:* and thou shalt go down *the tubes (but not the Fallopian ones) from listening to and endorsing all the irrelevant academic, scientific and religious, crap you've experienced and suffered,* and be lower *in cultural/social status as a direct result of your wayward impudence.*

He shall lend to thee, and thou shalt not lend to Him. He shall *as the Master Creator* be as the *coin* head, and thou shalt be the *opposite coin* tail, *that is, if you both continue to act and behave like mule-headed asses and stubborn-assed donkeys.*

164

And all these *wondrous* curses shall *miraculously* come upon thee, and shall pursue and overtake thee *all the way from womb to tomb,* till thou *finally* perish *from the Grim Reaper's swift swipe:* because thou heardst not the Voice of the Lord thy God, *so I (Moses) hereby warn you Israelite traitor, never become deaf (of the Lord's Commandments) if you have any idea what's fuckin' good for you.* And didst thou not keep His *Superlative* Commandments and ceremonies which He had *sympathetically* commanded thee, *and if not, then you might as well commence with your quick and abrupt suicide right here and now.*

And they shall be as signs and *woeful* wonders on thee, and on thy *tarnished* seed forever, *which in truth might never end.* Because thou didst not *obediently* serve the Lord thy God with joy and gladness of heart, for the abundance of all things *He never gave you that which you and your inferior ilk have stolen from the pagans and from the heathens, and from the gentle gentiles, along with the other numerous donkey cart vigilante gangs roaming the dirt streets and furthermore, terrorizing the dusty trails out there in uncharted territory. And in like manner, Oz (Og) never gave anything to the Tin Man, that he didn't already have!*

For the dozenth damned time, as a penalty thou shalt serve thy enemy, whom the Lord will send upon thee, in hunger, and thirst, and in *alluring* nakedness, and in want of all *material and immaterial* things you *now will soon possess:* and He shall put an iron yoke upon thy *pencil-shaped* neck, till He consume thee *in a frenzied cannibalistic reverse communion, angrily turning your entire body into edible graphite. Just continue your sinning and then watch all of this dramatic bullshit happen!*

The Lord will bring upon thee a *fearsome* nation from afar, and *coming* from the uttermost ends of the Earth, like a *hawk-eyed* eagle that flyeth swiftly, whose tongue thou canst not understand *because the voracious bird-brain has a hooked beak and can't communicate a fuckin' recognizable syllable intelligibly.*

A most insolent nation *is this' Defiant Israel, a stubborn people* that will show no regard to the *diaper-clad senile* ancients, nor have pity on the *helpless crying diseased* infants *that will surely evolve into the next generation of diaper-clad, senile, pissing and doddering elders.*

And locusts *from downtown Locust Street* will devour the fruit of thy cattle, *even though thy cattle solely munch and chew on grass and upon semi-nutritious weeds,* and *the angry Lord* will leave thee no wheat, *no wheat germ, no wheat germs,* nor wine, nor oil, *nor facial oil or soothing skin cream,* nor herds of oxen, nor flocks of sheep: until He destroys thee *because you foolishly failed to worship Him and because you failed to courteously honor His relatively elementary and simple (minded?) Ten Commandments. And folks, that's the gospel truth!*

And consume thee in all thy *corrupt* cities, *hovels* and *corresponding towns, you aberrant Israelite economic consumers,* and thy strong and high wall be brought down, *just like future London Bridges will be immobilized too.* And thou shalt eat the fruit of thy womb, *which is a fucked-up euphemism, or another fancy way of saying "licking and lapping available pussy,"* and the flesh of thy sons and of thy daughters, which the Lord thy God shall give thee *to sodomize and molest as if you were a neighborhood pedophile priest or a rural rabid rabbi,* in the distress and extremity wherewith thy enemy shall oppress thee, *namely after either being atrociously kicked in the balls or surprisingly castrated.*

The man that is nice among you, *better known as the tranquil gay guy,* and *he being* very delicate, *having and exhibiting despicable feminine ways,* shall envy his own straight *straight-dicked* brother, and his *brother's hairy cunt* wife, that lieth in his bosom, *because he (the straight brother) is now-pregnant again.*

So that he *(the now-pregnant husband-straight-brother)* will not give them *(the pagan cannibals)* of the flesh of his children, which he shall eat himself when hungry, *thus supporting his current pregnancy nutritional needs:* because he hath nothing else in the siege and in the want, wherewith thy *bitter* enemies shall distress thee within all thy gates, *those obstinate sage pagans that still control the general economy, not offering the now-pregnant husband any welfare, nor one iota of free day care, free lodging, free education or free food stamps.*

166

The tender and delicate *non-pregnant* woman *wife,* that could not go upon the ground *into a fox-hole and get laid by her now-pregnant husband,* nor set down her foot for over much niceness and tenderness *from the gay faggot brother-in-law,* will envy her *pregnant* husband who lieth in her bosom *as if he himself was a curled-up fetus,* the flesh of her son, and of her daughter. *Either that dumb illogical bullshit happening, or else the now-pregnant husband had been preparing to die all along, and the brain-dead shithead intends to be buried in the classic fetal position.*

And the filth *and stench* of the *bloody* afterbirths, that come forth from between her *(thy wife's)* hairy thighs, *and the children that are born the same hour from his (her pregnant husband's) womb (asshole), all twenty of those new born suckers that are born every three minutes according to my best chum adviser, P.T. Abraham.* For they' shall *evilly* eat them *(their newborn kids)* secretly for the want of all things, in the siege and distress, wherewith thy persistent *pagan and gay* enemy shall oppress thee within thy gates *and make your civilized survival difficult.*

If thou wilt not keep, and fulfill all the *questionable* words of this *insane* law, that are written *and interpreted* in this *infallible* volume, and fear His glorious and terrible Name: then the *relentless* Lord thy God shall increase thy plagues, and the plagues of thy *penalized* seed, *catastrophic* plagues, great and lasting, infirmities grievous and perpetual, *because these incredible supernatural mechanisms are the entire basis of our fucked-up religion, whether we like it or not.*

And He shall bring back on thee all the afflictions of Egypt, *including the dreaded S and M Bondage Chamber,* which thou wast afraid of *dying inside from an excess of masochistic pleasure,* and they *(these horrible S and M memories)* shall stick fast to thee *like white on rice and like brown on shit.*

Moreover the *merciless* Lord *(still studying how to be merciful while learning and mastering Morality, 101)* will bring upon thee all the *harmful* diseases, and *all* the *putrid* plagues, that are not written in the volume of this law, till He consumes thee f*or the freakin' twentieth time. In truth, I know about all this Biblical eating bullshit from reading a watered-down version of Consumer's Report.*

And you *Israel* shall remain few in number, who before were as *plentiful as* the *Cairo and Hollywood* stars, *and the many stars shining inside the evil zodiac constellations too,* because thou heardst not the Voice of the Lord thy God, *but instead, thou ardently tried figuring-out how the planets, stars, asteroids, hemorrhoids and solar system actually work.*

And as the Lord rejoiced upon you before doing good to you *by means of tough love retribution and agonizing persecution,* and multiplying you *without Him cruelly invoking the usual castration punishment:* so He shall rejoice destroying and bringing you to nought, so that you shall be taken away from the land which thou shalt go in to possess, *and regrettably, you will be eliminated (and not rewarded) from participating in the proposed fabulous Promised Land Manifest Destiny Land Grab that's now scribbled upon His personal drawing board.*

The Lord shall scatter thee *(every last cell, atom and molecule in your vile condemned body)* among all people, from the farthest parts of the Earth to the ends thereof, *which we don't have the required science and specific knowledge to ever presently determine:* and there thou shalt serve strange *Siberian, Swahili and Eskimo* gods, which both thou art ignorant of, and also *of which* thy *three deceased non-triplet fathers were not aware of,* false gods *made of holly* wood and *lava-ass-spewing* stone.

Neither shalt thou be quiet, even in those *conquered pagan* nations, *mum's the word, nor* shall *you ever experience* any rest for the sole of thy *infected* foot, *even if it heels (heals) over time.* For the Lord will give thee a fearful heart, and languishing *bloodshot* eyes, and a soul consumed with pensiveness, *and also sperm-less high balls filled with liquor.*

And thy *entire lackluster* life shall be as it were hanging before thee *like those sperm-less high balls filled with liquor.* Thou shalt fear night and day, *dawn and dusk,* neither shalt thou trust thy life *with potentially catastrophic twilight.*

In the morning thou shalt say *to no one:* "Who will grant me evening?" and at evening, *perhaps the ominous eerie midnight hour:* "Who will grant me morning?" for the fearfulness of thy *lambasted* heart, wherewith thou shalt be terrified, and for those things which thou shalt see with thy eyes, *all this amazing convoluted bullshit happening all because our fucked-up Old Testament Bible (and also our fucked-up Old Testament religion) is based on the anti-love founding principles of first creating emotional fear and then cruelly administering simultaneous human punishment.*

The Lord shall bring thee *(Israelite asshole)* again *across the vast arid desert* with *hard*ships *back* into Egypt, by the way whereof He *had previously* said to thee *(me, Moses)* that thou shouldst see it no more. There shalt thou be set to sale *(sail)* to thy pagan *straight and gay old Egyptian* enemies *for the purpose of you again becoming and* being bondmen and bondwomen, and I *(Moses)* predict that no man shall buy you *before you return for rehabilitation to the infamous Cairo S and M Bondage Clinic. I mean, after all those miserable years of Egyptian captivity, who the hell wants or needs more of that lousy, horrendous, unethical, immoral slave and torture shit?*

Chapter Twenty-nine

"Past Favors Recalled"

The *redundant* covenant is solemnly confirmed between God and His *(masculine by preference) disadvantaged* people. Threats against those that shall break it *are too fuckin' numerous to think about let alone be thoroughly mentioned. In case you dimwits haven't been paying close attention,* these are the words of the covenant which the Lord commanded Moses *(me)* to make with the children of Israel in the land of Moab *Dickie:* beside that covenant which He had made with them in Horeb, where I *(Moses) had impetuously broken the Lord's stones out of sheer psychological frustration.*

And I Moses, now *suffering from acute laryngitis that was not a mere cute cold,* called all Israel, and *predictably* said to them, *one million dumb fuck-heads strong:* "You have seen all the things that the Lord did before you in the land of Egypt to *the beleaguered anonymous* Pharaoh, and to all his *even more beleaguered anonymous incognito* servants, and to his *mostly beleaguered anonymous incognito* whole *devastated* land."

The great temptations, which thy' eyes have seen *and thy dicks and pussies have experienced first-hand,* those mighty signs and *sexual* wonders *must be avoided or else you erratic Israelites will be more than sorry for your great grievous sins.* And the Lord hath not given you a *cardiac-arrest* heart to understand, and *keen discerning* eyes to *instantly* see *and evaluate new sex opportunities,* and ears that may hear *pornography being read and recited through thy neighbor's open window, right* unto this present *fucked-up* day.

He hath brought you forty years through the desert *and hath graciously allowed you to live through the four decade misadventure against* your obdurate wills. Your *tawdry smelly* garments are not worn-out, *so therefore, you should wear your weatherworn rags inside-out.* Neither are the shoes of your feet consumed with age, *but your diseased lungs are definitely consumed with consumption. In terms of your callused feet and shoes (sandals), I recommend that you gingerly walk on your heels to save your meaningless soles!*

You' have not eaten bread, nor have you drunk wine, *nor have you drunk bread nor eaten wine or even tasted strong drink known as liquor:* that you might know that I am the Lord your God, *Who really doesn't care what you nomadic immigrants eat, drink, shit or fart.*

And you came to this *remote hideous* place: and Sehon King of Hesebon *Cinnebon, which has no synonym,* and Og, King *Wizard* of Basan *Basin, also known as Basin* Basan, came out against us to fight *what the two quacks believed to be the marauding alien Asssearians.* And we slew them *both without pause or hesitation.*

And we took their land, and delivered it for a possession to Reuben, *the area Sandwich King,* and to *both* Gad *and Egad, and also to the half tribe of* "Slow as Molasses" Manasses *and his Queen wife Virginia.*

Keep therefore the words of this covenant, and fulfill them: that you may understand all that you do *that is both wrong and sinful.* You all stand this day before the Lord your God, *Whom only I (Moses) can see and hear,* yes, your princes, and tribes, and your *incontinent* ancients, *all meandering around on this contiguous continent,* and *quack* doctors, *and* all the people of Israel, *none of whom pay taxes, rent, tribute or bills of any kind, except when the dimwits are enthusiastically patronizing the thriving bordellos, the booming sex parlors, along with the array of unisex tattoo and body mutilation boutiques.*

Your children and your wives, *of which some of you illegitimate nincompoops can't tell the difference, and the blithe gay delicate* stranger that abideth with thee in the camp *play room, doing sneaky voyeur stuff* besides *being* the hewers of *dildo* wood, *and then that the sinning homo' faggot inconspicuously brings to himself water to wash and cleanse his shaven asshole before being graphically (but not geographically) sodomized by horny sex-starved soldiers, both gay and straight gigolos.*

That thou mayst pass in the covenant of the Lord thy God, and in the oath which this day the Lord thy God maketh with thee, *I insist that you recalcitrant retards finally memorize and understand the simple Commandment language after reviewing over ten dozen insidious aggravating readings.*

That He *(the never fatigued Lord)* may raise thee up a people to Himself, *but not to create more gods on His exact same level who would evilly challenge His assumed authority,* and He may *(or honestly may not)* be thy God as He hath spoken to thee *through me* (Moses), *His personal translator and confidential interpreter,* and as He did swear to thy *three non-triplet biological fathers:* Abraham, Isaac, and Jacob.

Neither with you Israel only do I make this *vital* covenant, and confirm these *coveted* oaths, *even though ceremonial things like baptism and 'confirmation' are mere hypotheticals to be initiated and implemented sometime in the distant future.* But with all that are present *and all that are absent here today, I count three of you standing out there: the senile rabbi, the incontinent judge and the naked diaper-less pedophile priest.* For you *three assembled screwballs,* know *and remember* how we dwelt in the land of Egypt, and how we have passed through the midst of *misty* nations, and passing through them, *I have learned how to be God's select filter assigned to fully educate you. Why are you three ridiculous assholes all frenetically scratching your balls? Are you three ignoramuses all itching to get the hell out of here?*

You have seen their *(the Egyptians, just like the sinning pagans and the sinning heathens, although the sinning Egyptians are both of those vile things, heathens and pagans)* abominations and *assorted* filth, that is to say, their *impressive male* idols, wooden ones *with long carved wheeled wood peckers,* and stone ones, *having the entertaining hot lava assholes, lava dicks, and also I must mention the enchanting female images featuring fascinating and amusing lava tit' discharges, not to exclude* those other *contemptuous* statues of silver and gold, which they *(especially the wealthy Egyptians) religiously* worshiped.

Lest perhaps there should be among you a man or a woman, a family or a tribe, whose heart is turned away this day from the Lord our God *and influenced by these more sense-arousing matters and impertinent issues,* to go and serve the *false* gods of those nations *when you could get laid or sucked-off simply sinning right here in the almost uninhabitable Promised Land:* and there should be among you a root bringing forth gall *bladder* and *spleen-like* bitterness.

And when he *(you Israelite dumb bastards and bitches)* shall hear the words of this oath, he should *install an altar inside his/her chest* and bless himself/*herself* in his/*her* heart saying: "I shall have peace, *and yes, wanting, craving and desiring a good piece of ass, he/she* will walk on in the naughtiness of my heart: and the drunken may consume the thirsty. *Fuck only guzzling-down booze, you foul Israelites! You had wanted hot sizzling sex as your top priority all along!*

The drunken *fellow,* etc., absumat ebria sitientem... *(Translation: I really love sin and excessive pleasure. Give me more!)* It is a proverbial expression, which may either be understood, as spoken by the *common asshole* sinner, a *sort of inexplicable* blessing, that is, flattering himself in his *self-indulgent gratifying* sins with the *sinister* imagination of peace *of mind caused by encountering an illicit piece of ass,* and so great an abundance as may satisfy *your lustful anxiety* with *your silly erect genitalia flopping and maniacally throbbing up-and-down, the sinful process that causes you to think with your dick and not with your fucked-up brain, because all the essential cerebral blood is now in your former organ (dick) and not in your latter one (head).* "Oh Shit! *If only I (Moses) could muster one final three-inch-long hard-on and one tiny mostly-air ejaculation' penis discharge, just to make my miserable life a trifle more tolerable! Even a small fart out of my limp dick would be absolutely great! Hey P. T.! Where's my inflatable pagan girl doll you had promised me?"*

And the Lord should not forgive him: but His wrath and jealousy against that man should be exceedingly enkindled at that time, and all the curses that are written in this volume should light upon him: and the Lord should blot-out his name from under Heaven. *Now where's that damned blow-up pagan girl doll P.T.? I need some therapeutic physical comfort right this minute, before the jealous Lord arrives on the scene and blows-up my imaginary blow-up doll! My flagging self-esteem is being minimized!"*

And utterly destroy him out of all the tribes of Israel, according to the curses that are contained in the book of this *divine* law and

174

covenant. *"Who gives a shit any more about Biblical Deuteronomy! I'm thinking about doing something especially kinky with the imaginary pagan inflatable carnival doll!"*

And the following generation shall say, and the children that shall be born hereafter, and the strangers that shall come from afar, seeing the plagues of that land and the evils wherewith. *"Shit! The all-too-tricky Lord hath intercepted my private thought patterns and hath afflicted the whole damned Earth with ten million inflatable gay lesbian and trans-gender transvestite carnival dolls! What a friggin' holocaust this infuriating nutcase bullshit has turned-out to be!*

Burning it *(who gives a rat's ass what the hell "it" is that's wildly burning!)* with brimstone, and the heat of salt *and pepper,* so that it cannot be sown *or sewn* any more, nor any green thing *like a frog or a snake* grow *from the soil* therein, after the example of the destruction of Sodom and Gomorrah, Adama and Seboim, *four popular tourist towns* which the Lord had *magnificently* destroyed in His wrath and indignation because they *(their bored populations, both male and female) were desperately searching the hot arid desert wilderness looking for rare inflatable straight and gay used pagan carnival dolls!*

And all the nations shall say: "Why hath the Lord done thus to this *once popular inflatable pagan doll tourist-trap* land? What meaneth this exceedingly great heat of His wrath, *except that maybe He despises the new fabric material known as rubber?"*

And they *(whoever is left in the ever-diminishing audience)* shall answer: "Because they forsook the Covenant of the Lord, which He had made *with their three non-triplet biological deceased fathers,* when He brought them *(the wandering Israelites, not their three deceased non-triplet deceased fathers)* out of the land of Egypt." *And next the robotic masses discontinue their chant, all departing the scene in unison. "Holy smokes! Now there's just one dumb-ass person left in the audience, me, the ignored speaker, Moses! Great balls of fire! There's an intense meteor attack that's flaming -up the whole visible atmosphere!"*

And they *(the million Israelites who had promptly departed the audience)* have served strange gods, *stranger than fiction deities,* and

175

hath adored them, *especially their flaming lava-filled (emitting and shooting) assholes,* whom they knew not, and for whom they had not been assigned *a volcano warning and an emergency go-to safety station.*

Therefore the wrath of the Lord was kindled against this land's *limited meager supply of wood,* to bring upon it all the curses that are written in this *somewhat phenomenal* volume, *including His magical confiscation of all the fuckin' inflatable rubber pagan carnival dolls.*

And He hath cast them *(the blow-up sideshow dolls, the pagans and the Israelites)* out of their land, in anger and in wrath, and in very great indignation, and hath thrown them into a strange land *having only gay, lesbian and trans-gender transvestite puppets and oddball marionettes,* as it is seen this *very sad* day *in the disappointing establishment of the City of Godville.*

Secret things to the Lord our God: things that are manifest, to us and to our children forever, that we may do all the words of this *especially demanding, unrealistic, impractical* law. Look Lord! *Please grant me an inflatable pagan girl carnival doll that's recently gone through puberty, or better yet, send me to where I could find a nice one with a fluffy brown bush and big hard tits and a firm ass too; yes, happy me (Moses) being all alone in* the *hot formidable Sinai Desert with my precious treasured rubber pagan girl carnival toy! I'll even settle for an inflatable gay camel to play around with at this ugly stage of the all-too-cruel aging game!*

176

Chapter Thirty

"Mercy for the Repentant"

Great mercies *(even in France)* are promised to the penitent: God's Commandment is *quite* feasible. *Another Biblical assumption is that* life and death are *predestined and are* set before them *(the Chosen People for the Chosen Promised Land).* Now when all these *undefined and unidentified* things shall come upon thee *like a ton of stench-laden horse manure,* either the blessing or the curse, which I have *futilely* set forth before thee *thick-skulled lunk-heads thousands of times,* and thou shalt be touched with repentance of thy heart among all the *sinning* nations, into which the Lord thy God shall have scattered thee, *limb by limb, molecule by molecule, the repentant shall be forgiven for any crime or committed sin, regardless of magnitude or degree, as long as he (or she, but always masculine by preference) is repentant to the Lord.*

And shalt return to *Omnipotent* Him, and obey His Ten Commandments, as I command thee *along with the three senile geriatric assholes* this *very significant* day, *all three of you doddering, slobbering, diaper-pissing unconscious idiots,* thou and thy *always also-pissing* children, *many already in yellow-stained diapers at age ten,* with all thy heart, and with all thy *dumb-fuck* soul. *Indeed, after Heaven and Hell for human souls are finally established, the population for Heaven is going to be four, and everyone else is going to be lodged in the raging inferno lava pits hastily constructed down below. Magma and molten volcanic rock will be in all the condemned place's steaming-hot swimming pools, spewing sulfur springs and belching-burning recreational lakes. No wonder why Heaven is (and will be) regarded as "Fabulous Paradise" compared to that scary Hell scenario shit.*

The Lord thy God, *enjoying playing solitaire power games with human pawns on His elaborate game board,* will bring back again thy Captivity, and will have 'mercy' on thee *if you hapless itinerant parasites journey all the way to Paris,* and He will gather thee *(the hapless Jews)* again out of all the nations *that wanted to get rid of you simpleton fuck-heads centuries before yesterday,* into which He had scattered thee before, *His inflexible rigid philosophy succinctly* being, *"My Holy Way or the punishment/captivity highway, you roguish nimrods!"*

If thou be driven as far as the poles of Heaven, the Lord thy God will fetch thee back from hence, *not wanting to see you become as bipolar as He is.* And He will take thee to Himself, and bring thee into the *pledged* land which thy *three possessed deceased non-triplet biological* fathers *had irrationally* possessed, and thou shalt possess it, *because possession is nine-tenths of the Holy Law,* and blessing thee, He will make thee more numerous than were thy *three non-triplet originally impotent* fathers.

But the Lord must have blessed the more culturally advanced Egyptians and the more knowledgeable Mesopotamians much greater than He had graced us lowlife Jews, because there are millions more of those fucked-up alien pagan assholes traveling around and trekking through our habitat region than there are nomadic Hebrew tribesmen, all lost and still wandering in concentric circles for forty additional years, traversing the Sinai Desert for the fourth time following a delusional power-hungry Old Fart like stupid-ass me (Miserable Moses).

The Lord thy God will circumcise thy heart *like the senile rabbi has done to our tender dicks' at age fifty-five,* and the heart of thy *unfortunate* seed too, *so even tiny sperms will be circumcised too: maybe ovary eggs will get the dreaded scalpel treatment also? Who the hell knows or cares?*

And He will turn all these *numerous* curses upon thy' enemies, and upon them that hate and persecute thee. *And after that particular fiasco is fully enacted, He will then turn the horrid curses back upon isolated Israel, whimsically playing a nifty-type ping-pong game with our individual fates and with our accursed tribal destiny hanging in the balance.*

But thou shalt return *like obedient slaves to His controversial fickle wish,* and listen to the *constructive* Voice of the Lord thy God, *that only I Moses can hear once in a while during a very rare purple moon eclipse,* and shalt do all the Commandments which I command thee this *memorable* day, *or else live the pathetic, melancholy lackluster life of a mortal pawn ping -pong ball.*

And the *awe-inspiring* Lord thy God will make thee abound in all the works of thy *lazy cumbersome* hands, in the fruit of thy womb, *you callow shallow men will find vegetables also in your newly installed uteruses,* and in the fruit of thy cattle *that only chew yellow grass and lavender wild weeds,* in the fruitfulness of thy *desolate desert* land, and in the plenty of all *wonderful* things, *except the gay faggot fruits and fruitcakes that mostly hang-out (when their minuscule testicles hang-out) at the local bizarre bazaar on Saturday nights, looking for immediate hits.* For the Lord will return to rejoice over thee in all good things, as He rejoiced in thy three *dead non-triplet biological* fathers *several lost centuries ago.*

Yet so if thou hear the *distinctive* Voice of the Lord thy God, *suspect that you are becoming delusional just like myself,* and keep His *essential* precepts and *His zany sacrificial* ceremonies, which are written *in disarray with*in this *unworkable dysfunctional* law: *and even if you can't fly-up to* Heaven *like the jet-propelled archangels do,* return to the Lord thy God with all thy heart, and with all thy *troubled* soul.

This Commandment, that I command thee this *relevant* day, is not above thee, nor far off from thee: Nor is it in Heaven, *where no mundane rules are needed,* that thou shouldst *stupidly* say *to me:* "Which of us can go up to Heaven to bring it unto us, and we may hear and fulfill it in work *and deed? Asshole Old Fart bullshit artist Moses, do you see any fuckin' wings on our scrawny backs? Are you blind besides being abundantly daft?"*

Nor is it *somewhere* beyond the sea: that thou mayst excuse thyself, and *idiotically* say: "Which of us can cross the *deep blue* sea, and *therefore* bring it unto us: that we may hear, and do that which is commanded? *We can't even get across the damned Jordan Torrent let alone across a friggin' local sea or sailing a colossal mythological ocean! Old Fart Moses, are you again totally wacky? Your asinine bullshit is enough to make a grown man groan and then quickly change his totally implausible religion!"*

But the word is very nigh unto thee, in thy mouth and in thy *un-spirited* heart, that thou mayst do it *out of fear of getting your dirty asshole cauterized from Above, not by the vile Ass-searians, but by the Lord's legendary mighty high-energy lightning bolts.*

179

Consider that I have set before thee this day life and good on one hand, and on the other *hand, the sinister one that is left,* death and evil. *Now then, simply imagine that your left hand has been amputated, and you now can only utilize your more appropriate right appendage. Grow a brain Israelites! It's all that freakin' simple to understand!*

That thou mayst love the Lord thy God, and walk in His *unknown mysterious* ways, and keep His Commandments along with *His zany sacrificial* ceremonies and *His very ludicrous, very questionable, very objectionable zesty* judgments *too,* and bless thee in the *invaded conquered* land, which thou shalt go in to *greedily* possess *for the ten millionth time.*

But if thy heart be turned away, *that is, radically reversed inside thy chest cavity,* so that thou wilt not 'hear', and being deceived with error, thou adore strange gods, and serve them *in their convent cafeterias, then you zany Israelite don't deserve to have a set of ears situated inside your reversed heart chambers.*

I *(Moses)* foretell thee this day that thou shalt perish, and shalt remain but a short time in the *pertinent transitional* land, to which thou shalt pass-over the River Jordan *in honor of the Passover,* and shalt go in to possess the Promised Land *that even the fucked-up pagan inhabitants absolutely loathe and abhor.*

I call *upon* Heaven and Earth (*without the requisite aid of a future device that will be conveniently named "telephone"*) to witness this day, *for when I speak or call, I (Venerable Moses) can then eventually see better. The* ten laws that I have set before you will make you decide between life and death, between blessing and cursing, *between being able to only jerk-off with your right hand because your left one has been amputated.* Choose therefore life *and jerking-off or masturbating with your right hand,* that both thou and thy seed may live, *but since no Heaven or Hell exists yet for us pathetic puny humans, in death, it (the rational choice) really doesn't fuckin' matter one iota.*

And that thou mayst love the Lord thy God, and *responsibly* obey His *invisible, indiscernible mystic* Voice *that only I Moses can recognize and hear,* and adhere to Him as if He were sticky *flypaper* (for He is thy life, and the *full* length of thy *accursed doomed* days), that thou, *in a somber frame of mind,* mayst dwell in the *infertile, inhospitable, deplorable* Promised Land *that's already quite overcrowded and overpopulated with all sorts of deranged pagans, heathens, prophets, gentiles along with a multitude of gay, transgender and lesbian LBTG knuckleheads.*

Chapter Thirty-one

"The Lord's Leadership"

Moses *(me)* encourageth the *apathetic* people', and Josue *too, who is appointed to succeed him (me), and had been assigned by the Lord through me to learn and master all of the necessary problematic religious Biblical background bullshit that is required in my job description.* He delivereth the law to the *incontinent* priests, *who thought that Josue was actually delivering new fresh clean diapers and a brand new invention to replace common staffs, certain novel newly improvised things called canes.*

God foretelleth that the *disinterested* people will often forsake him *(Josue), and so my very capable successor Josue will quickly punish* them *(the obdurate dumb-ass fickle-minded people) by blowing hard into his trumpet ram horn and effectively shattering their eardrums while tooting his ultra-shrill high notes.* He *(the demanding Lord)* commandeth Moses *(me)* to write a *two-paragraph* canticle, as a constant remembrance *of the convoluted dysfunctional imperative Ten Commandment law. But since writing has not been devised yet, this most recent impractical demand represented an impossible false request.*

And Moses *(that's me folks)* went, and spoke all these *fantastic incredible* words to all Israel, and everyone assembled *in the volatile audience* kept yelling in unison, *"Bullshit, bullshit, bullshit!"* And I *(Moses) valiantly* said to them: "I am this day a hundred and twenty years old; I can no longer go out and come in, *and I have trouble finding my shriveled-up dick to take a piss, and I can't reach my ass to hastily wipe it with cactus parts after suffering through another constipated dump.* Especially as the Lord' also hath said to me *in private secure telepathic communication:* "Moses, Thou shalt not pass over this River Jordan *before the next big Passover celebration! Do I' make Myself' clear?"*

The Lord thy God then will pass over before thee *Josue, despite the recent Passover celebration allusion thing:* He will destroy all these *opposing hostile* nations in thy sight, and thou shalt possess them *to both exploit and enslave your hostages:* and this *dear* Josue shall go over before thee, as the Lord hath spoken to me *during one of my regular paranoid delusional nightmares. Angel of Death, please hurry with initiating your important mission!*

And the Lord shall do to them as he did to Sehon and to Og *the Wizard King,* and to the kings of the *amorous* Amorrhites, and to their *forsaken* land, and *He* shall *violently* destroy them *as is His favorite fun pastime hobby.* Therefore when the *on-a-mission* Lord shall have delivered these *prize victories* also to you *(Josue),* you shall do in like manner to them as I have commanded you *and mercilessly execute the pagans, the heathens, the gentle* gentile, *the licentious lesbians, the gay faggot infidels and the gay faggot heathens too, and let's not forget the very dangerous lecherous transgender and transvestite freakos.*

Do manfully and be of good heart *Josue: keep learning the fine art of blasting loud noise from the trumpet horn,* and fear not *playing solo musical appearances before the mindless huddling Israelite masses,* nor be ye dismayed at their *unkempt derelict* sight: for the *indispensable* Lord thy God, *He Himself is thy Leader Who incidentally often practices playing the tenor saxophone,* and will not leave thee nor *permanently* forsake thee. In fact my *dear Josue, He, Michael and Gabriel are in the process of forming an exclusive musical instrumental trio as I speak.*

And Moses *(1)* called *upon* Josue *from his rather rudimentary pyramid-shaped tent,* and said to him before all the *sluggish languid* Israelites, *most of whom were snoring loudly with their bleary eyes fully open:* "Take courage, and be valiant: for thou shalt bring this *lazy fucked-up dumbbell* people into the land which the Lord swore *upon His first saxophone* that He would give *the worthless territory* to their *three non-triplet deceased biological* fathers, and thou *Josue* shalt *honorably* divide it by *lots of* lots *to Lot's descendants.*

And the Lord, Who is your *brand new jazz band* Leader, He Himself will be with thee *when thy dynamically blow thy trumpet horn:* He will not leave thee, nor forsake thee: fear not *Josue,* neither be *ye* dismayed *by all this superfluous information, because if He likes what He hears from your loud ear-shattering horn blasts, you might ultimately qualify being asked to join His secretly planned jazz quartet.*

And Moses *(Me)* hastily jotted-down *(scribbled in lower-glyphics)* this *jumbled* law, and *next* delivered it to the *incontinent* priests *who also doubled as* the *blue denim* sons of *laconic* Levi, who *had* carried the Ark of the Covenant of the Lord *all the way from Noah's house in Syria, or perhaps the dwelling was located in Mesopotamia, and brought* it *(the Ark)* to all the *diapered* ancients of Israel, *who erroneously thought that the precious sacred ark was a new kind of public urinal.*

And *reticent* he *(the incontinent piss-poor Levi priest)* commanded them *(anyone who happened to be there),* saying: "After seven *stressful* years, in the year of remission, in the feast of tabernacles, *we all should be free of our cancers and of our itchy venereal diseases! Hey, someone please get those nasty, despicable tent caterpillars off of the damned tabernacle!"*

When all Israel *finally* come together, to appear in the sight of the Lord thy God in the *new* place *referred to as Godville,* which the Lord shall choose *a location for someday,* thou *(Josue)* shalt read the words of this *confusing hypocritical* law before all Israel, in their hearing. *"But Josue, first you fuckin' gotta' learn how to read, you retarded hundred year old illiterate! And besides that glaring fact, essential alphabets and writing haven't been invented yet!"*

And the *indolent, phlegmatic, lethargic, obdurate* people being all assembled together *to hear our dual incredulous bullshit being shouted at them again,* both men and women, children and *a giggling gaggle of delicate* LBGT strangers, *those lawless event crashers* that are within thy gates *without having authentic admission stubs:* that hearing *our combined propaganda nonsense,* that they may learn *some interesting Biblical mythology,* and *consequently* fear the Lord your God *and His traveling three piece trio,* and keep and fulfill all the *hypocritical* words of this *inflexible dictatorial* Ten Commandment law.

That their children also, who now are *equally as* ignorant *as they are,* may hear, and *also* fear the Lord their God *and His formidable traveling trio,* all the days that they live in the *lousy* land; whither you are going over the Jordan to possess it, *remember that the Lord, Angel Michael and fearsome ill-tempered Gabriel might be instrumental in causing your sudden demise, their clamorous supersonic music causing you to instantly become comatose and brain dead!*

And the Lord *next* said to Moses *(me):* "Behold *and not be held!* The days of thy *imminent* death are nigh: *I suggest that you* call that *talented musician* Josue, and stand ye in the *tattered* tabernacle tent of the testimony, that I may give him a charge *of electricity in a pottery bottle designed to keep you alive a little longer. And Moses, get those slimy tent caterpillars out of My sacred tabernacle!"*

So Moses *(me)* and Josue went and stood in the tabernacle *tent* of the testimony, *both of us gullible mortal fools waiting to experience something rather electrifying.* And the Lord appeared *and manifested Himself* there atop the *center* pillar of a cloud, *but only I saw and heard Him. And the foggy blurry pillar* stood *and then creatively danced* in the entry of the tabernacle, *the celestial cloud column symbolically suggesting that Josue and I were regarded by Heaven as both being pillars of the Jewish community.*

And the Lord said to Moses *(me):* "Behold thou shalt *soon* sleep with thy *lifeless three dead* fathers, and this *rebel-rousing* people rising-up will go a-fornicating after *worshiping* strange *lava-ass* gods *that abound* in the land, to which it goeth in to dwell: there, and *then the clown-oriented buffoons* will forsake Me, and will make void the covenant, which I have made with them *even before I took-up playing the tenor saxophone."*

"And My *fierce* wrath shall be kindled against their *skinny buttocks* in that day: and I will forsake them and their *deviate frivolous fancies,* and will *deliberately* hide My *awesome fearsome* face from them, and they shall then be *voraciously* devoured by *lesbian cannibals:* all *imaginable* evils and afflictions shall find them, so that the Israelites shall say in that day: 'In truth, it is because God is not with me, that these *myriad* evils have found me. *Why couldn't He take-up playing the sexophone instead of playing the very dreaded dreadful tenor saxophone'?"*

"But Decrepit Moses, I will hide, and cover My face in that day *with ample vanishing cream being applied so that It is not to be seen,* for all the evils which they *(the quarrelsome Hebrew idiots)* have

186

done, because they have followed strange gods *even stranger than thy egotistical Lord.*"

Now therefore, *thanks to great progress, we're (Moses and the gang) now up to ten letters in our antiquated Hebrew alphabet;* write you this *short* canticle, and teach the children of Israel, *all of them brave Josue, all by yourself:* that they may know it by heart *without using the dangerous brain,* and sing it by mouth, *throat and larynx too,* and this *fine* song may be unto me *(Holy Moses)* for a testimony among the children of Israel, *who just like their 'Don't give a shit!' ancestors and parents, the juvenile delinquent punk brats 'Don't give a shit!' either.*

For I will bring them *(parents and punk juvenile delinquent kids)* into the *Promised* Land, for which I swore to their *three non-triplet biological deceased* fathers *during the height of the Stone Age,* that floweth-over with *cow-less* milk and *bee-less* honey. And when they have eaten *neither commodity,* and are full and fat *and continuously farting their Hebrew asses off, they will also fart away their lives,* turn away *and go* after strange *demonic* gods, *honoring selfish human nature,* and *the dunce-headed imbeciles* will serve them *(other hot lava-pissing and lava-shitting false gods):* and the *deviate shit-head* Hebrews will despise me *(Moses),* and make void *(and avoid)* my *lifelong* covenant. *Josue baby, the misadventure's all up to you now!*

And after many more *terrible* evils *(created and sent by the Capricious Lord)* and *multiple harsh* afflictions shall have come upon them *(the whole "Don't give a shit!" reticent crowd),* this *abbreviated* canticle shall answer them *with a simulated Voice coming-up from the papyrus paper* for a *dramatic* testimony, which no oblivion shall take away out of the mouth of their *talking* seed *(speaking sperms).* For I *alone* know *the essence of* their greedy *selfish thoughts, because when I (Moses) was a young buck back in Egypt, I used to 'sell fish' and practice greed too in order to earn a buck,* and what they *(the Jewish retards)* are about to do this *historic* day, before that I bring them into the *cow-less and bee-less* Land of Milk and Honey, which I have *repeatedly and selfishly* promised them *from my mental tienda (brain store).*

Moses (me) therefore wrote the *brief* canticle, *which took five weeks to organize the three short paragraphs,* and *futilely* taught it to the *'Don't give a shit!' obnoxious delinquent* children of Israel. *To perform this most difficult function, I had to exhaust my ancient brain and imaginatively invent the Hebrew alphabet!*

And the Lord commanded Josue, the son of Nun *and the Senile Pedophile Priest,* and *loudly* said *through His tenor saxophone:* "Take courage, and be valiant *gallant Josue:* for thou shalt bring the children of Israel into the land which I have promised, and I will be with thee *playing my brass instrument in our new jazz quartet. Welcome aboard to the jazzed-up Old Testament team!"*

Therefore Moses *(I, me) was not interested in all that jazz and just wanted to die,* so after Moses *(I, me)* had wrote *(had written)* the words of this *incongruous meaningless* law *addressed to Josue and the Levites (a future jazz jam group)* in a *poorly constructed grammatical* volume, and finally finished it *(the easy essay composition) in another five short weeks.*

I then told my successor Josue: "Take this book, *and do not burn it by shoving it up the volcanic ass of a pagan statue that's still spewing molten lava.* Put it in the side of the Ark of the Covenant of the Lord your God, *which as you know is shaped and modeled after Noah's ark and in design looks something like a primitive prehistoric fishing boat:* that it may be there for a testimony against thee if it *(the ark and the written brief canticle) has to later testify in the senile judges' piss-stained courtroom."*

For I *(Moses)* know thy obstinacy, and thy most stiff neck, *of which you redneck hick Israelites possess.* While I am yet living *and still breathing once every three minutes,* and going in *(the cow-less, bee-less Promised Land)* with you, *I maintain that* you have always been rebellious against the Lord, *trying to start a Civil War amongst us over your' former and current slavery status:* How much more *shall this stupid shit continue* when I shall *gladly* be dead *and be finally liberated from all this ongoing petty human conflict bullshit?*

Gather unto me all the *yellow-diapered* ancients of your *belligerent* tribes, and your *quack* doctors, *and your quack ducks too,* and I will speak these *same disorganized confusing* words in their hearing, and will call *upon earless* Heaven and *brain-dead* Earth to witness against them.

For I know that, after my *much-anticipated and much welcomed approaching* death, you *creatures of bad habits* will do wickedly again, and deliberately ignoring my delusions and my strange mental manifestations, will quickly turn aside from the way that I *(Psychotic Moses)* have commanded you *hopeless immoral dolts:* and evils shall *again* come upon you in the latter times, *because that's the Lord's basic coping mechanism to realistically deal with you preposterous foolhardy assholes; and* when you shall do evil in the sight of the Lord, to provoke Him by the works of your *grubby grimy* hands, *you piss both Him and me off greatly. Are you paying attention and learning how I do this verbal bullshit Josue?*

Moses *(me)* therefore *eloquently* spoke *in a coarse hoarse tone of* voice, *lecturing* in the hearing of the whole assembly of Israel, the *fucked-up peculiar* words of this *most peculiar* canticle, and finished it *to the end in less than twenty-four hours record time, and at the important speech's climactic conclusion, only the three loyal yellow-diapered senile elders remained in the audience to hear the lengthy dissertation's very boring ending.*

Chapter Thirty-two

"The Song of Moses"

A *brief subtle* canticle *recited* for the *expressed* remembrance of the Ten Commandment law: Moses *(Me)* is commanded to go up into a *(unknown)* mountain, from whence, *without binoculars or a functional spyglass,* he shall see the Promised Land but not enter into it *by jumping-off the high summit and then flying ten miles to finally reach the long-desired destination.*

Hear, O ye Heavens, the things I *(Moses)* speak, *for I occasionally utter things and not words;* let the Earth give ear to the words *(things)* of my mouth. Let my doctrine gather as the rain *drowns the ants and slow-moving snails during a flash flood,* and let my speech distill as the dew *evaporates into nothing,* as a *baby* shower upon the herb, and as *tear* drops upon the *already saturated* grass.

Because I will invoke the name of the Lord: give ye magnificence *that none of you contemptuous reprehensible assholes have ever given homage* to our God. The works of God are perfect, and all His ways are judgments *that the diapered senile judges can neither fathom' or imagine: Unlike you less-than-mediocre nomadic nutcases,* God is faithful and without any iniquity; He is just and *just simply* right *all the friggin' time. The Lord hath wisdom that transcends mankind's fraudulent learned knowledge. That's why knowledge in the form of science and technology is fundamentally detrimental to our emotional and spiritual health.*

They *(you Hebrew fools and you deviate pagan shit-heads too)* have sinned against Him, and thou *are disowned and now* are none of His children, *all cavorting and traipsing around* in their *despicable* filth: *Amen,* they are a wicked and perverse *younger* generation *that effectively generates mass misery among the doomed remainder of us.*

Is this the return *on investment* thou makest to the Lord, O foolish and senseless *fucked-up* people? *Forget about the deceased non-triplets, Abraham, Isaac and Jacob.* Is not He thy Father', that hath possessed thee, and made thee, and created thee *without ever using sperms and eggs?*

Remember the *fond* days of old; think upon every *squandering* generation: ask thy *indolent lazy* father, and he will *indulgently* declare to thee: *and to* thy *senile diaper-pissing elders, and they' (the bald-headed, fat, doddering, slobbering savants and sages)* will *also* tell thee *the God's honest truth that we persist in forgetting.*

When the Most High divided the *most low'* nations: *yes, that was* when He separated the *Siamese twin sons* of Adam *with a lethal battle axe; Abel worked hard, but Cain was not able. Later,* He (the *discriminating judgmental* Lord) appointed *(and disappointed)* the bounds of people, according to the *unknown* number of the children of Israel, *the only nation in the whole wide world that remarkably gives birth to its own children without ever having any sex with any other nation.*

But the Lord's portion is his people: Jacob *being* the *real estate* lot of his inheritance. He *(the Omnipotent Lord)* found him *(Jacob, descendant of Lot) kneeling and crying for emergency medical help* in a desert land, *indeed* in a *scorpion and rattlesnake* place of *absolute* horror, and *an area* of vast *wild* wilderness *too:* He *(the Lord)* led him *(lost Jacob)* about *the thorny cactus patches to a Joshua tree, and taught him (Jacob) algebra, geometry and advanced trigonometry in addition to the Old Testament Bible Book of Genesis:* and He *(the Lord)* kept him *(Jacob)* as the apple of His eye *(apples of His eyes), predicting to Jacob that a military leader named Joshua (Josue) would someday emerge from obscurity and lead Israel to triumph in the Promised Land. Then the short-attention-spanned Lord promptly left the vicinity of the singular desert Joshua tree, and Jacob remained there on his sandy knees, crying and wailing even more intensely than he had been weeping before the compassionate Lord had showed-up to comfort him.*

As the eagle entices her young to fly *by talon-kicking them out of the high perched nest,* and then hovering over them *when they crash and impact upon the solid ground,* He *(Jacob, who had magically turned into an eagle)* spread his wings, and hath taken-off *on his new career as God's main bewildered prophet, circling around in the vast wilderness. So too will Josue fly like an eagle just as Stephen the village Miller had once done, but without magically turning into a feathered one like Jacob had achieved, unless Josue winds-up preaching Aviary over in Philadelphia, that eagle-loving city squarely situated in uncivilized pagan Palestine.*

The Lord alone was his *(Jacob's)* Fearless Leader: and there was no strange god with him *other than the Impeccable Lord.* He *(the Impeccable Lord)* set him *(Jacob, the new non-Philadelphia eagle)* upon high land *up in the highlands:* that he might eat the fruits of the *barren fallow* fields; that he *(Jacob)* might *lustily* suck honey out of the rock *after smoking his last itty-bitty marijuana joint,* and *then* suck oil out of the hardest stone, *and then try very hard to discover petroleum, because the word 'petroleum' actually means "from rock."*

They *(the local highland cliff dwellers)* provoked him *(Jacob)* by *invoking* strange gods, and stirred him up to anger with their *tempting* abominations. They *incessantly* sacrificed to devils, *to Philadelphia eagles,* and not to the Lord God: *but instead they sacrificed* to gods whom they knew not before: *gods* that were newly come up, whom their *callow lowbrow* fathers worshiped not, *new gods having the tantalizing names Baal, Balling, Lava, Pornography, Lesbia, Homo' Homo', Trans-Vestor and Pedophile Philadelphia Eagle.*

Thou hast forsaken the Lord God that begot thee *Jacob,* and thou hast forgotten the Lord that created thee, *even though Abraham was your grandfather and Isaac was your fertile pappy.*

The Lord saw *all this false god pageantry display,* and *as usual,* was *instantaneously* moved to wrath *and jealousy:* because His own *adopted* sons and daughters *(along with ancient Jacob)* had provoked Him *by arrogantly worshiping eagles in Philadelphia.*

And He *(the Omnipotent Lord)* said *(repeated):* "I will hide My face from them *as is My stealthy habit when I am angry,* and will *pensively* consider what their last end shall be: *I only wish now that Philadelphia was inside my divine jurisdiction so that I could get instant revenge* on this perverse generation of unfaithful children. *When I (the Lord) get the opportunity, I shall destroy their vanities, and their sinks, their bath tubs, their toilets, their makeshift shower heads and their rotting termite-infested kitchen cabinets too!"*

A fire is kindled in My' *(the Lord's)* wrath, and shall burn even to the lowest hell, *once I decide to invent Hell and then give all the Hebrew violators well-deserved real hell.* And *my raging fire shall* devour the Earth with her *(its)* increase, and shall burn the foundations of the mountains. *Even Jacob's several remaining Charity Foundations will be incinerated too! And* I will heap *a heap* of evils upon them *(Hebrew sinners),* and will spend My arrows among them *until Michael and Gabriel eventually manufacture for Me a better more modern archery set, or else I'll instantaneously make them both quiver.*

After being consumed with My fiery inferno anger tirades, they *(the aberrant Hebrew debauchers)* shall be *re*-consumed with famine, and *voracious* birds shall, *after drinking undiluted vinegar,* devour them with a most bitter bite: I will send the teeth of beasts *(without any accompanying dental records)* upon them, with the fury of creatures *like ordinary lambs and sheep* that trail upon the ground, *and with the amplified rage of cowardly yellow-bellied serpents and fierce attacking garden snakes, too.*

The sword shall lay them waste, and terror within *their cities,* both the young man and the virgin, the sucking child with the man in years, *all those vile Hebrew violators shall die by means of My' advanced cutting edge technology that Michael and Gabriel are assiduously developing along with the advanced archery arrows.*

I *(the jealous Formidable Lord)* said: Where are they? *(the fake false gods and their new-found worshipers, who used to be My rebellious congregation). Are they playing hide and seek?* I will make the memory of them *(the false gods with the lava-shooting erratic assholes)* to cease from among men, *even the young betrayers who used to proudly be My molested synagogue altar boys and My happy and gay castrated castrati choir soprano fags.*

But for the wrath of My' *traitorous betraying* enemies, I have deferred it *(My incisive and decisive retribution upon the molested faggot altar boys and the LBTG sopranos too):* lest perhaps their enemies might be proud *to molest them also, just like the senile* rabbis and the pervasive pedophile priests do religiously in My wholly holy places of worship.

They *(all the dumb-shit fucked-up Israelites)* are a nation without counsel *or guidance, and without wisdom, truth, honesty, logic, candor, poetry, courtesy, humanity, religion, morality, ethics, responsibility, integrity, dignity, trust, devout un-adulterated love, friendship, modesty, humility, fraternity, compassion, sympathy, justice, education, just to name a few worthwhile abstractions.*

O that they *(the fucked-up wandering clannish tribal Jews of both then, now and yesteryear)* would be wise and would understand, and would provide for their *dead-end* last end. How should one *(prophet, Moses)* pursue after a thousand *slugs and turtles (the doltish mentally challenged pea-brained Israelites),* and then two pursuers *(prophets, Moses and newcomer Josue)* chase ten thousand *slugging ninja turtles? What a fucked-up marathon sprint that epic theoretical bullshit misadventure would be!*

For our God is not as their *weirdo* gods: *their false gods are made of silver and gold, and our Lord (and me, Moses) desires to acquire silver and gold;* our *real* enemies themselves are the *pious, diaper-wetting senile Levite priests and those doddering diaper-pissing pagan* judges.

Their vines are of the vineyard of Sodom, and of the suburbs of Gomorrah: their grapes are grapes of gall, and their clusters most bitter. *I (the Lord) know this local gossip because I hear it on the religious grapevine from a minor gay prophet named Marvin.* Their wine is the gall of dragons, and the venom of asps, which is *virtually* incurable, *simply because it's impossible to kick an asps' ass in that an asp doesn't have any obvious, obese ass to kick.*

The Lord *will someday destroy all the senile liberal judges and then* judge His people all by Himself, and will have mercy on His servants, *Michael and Gabriel, but that scuttlebutt doesn't really matter since those two accomplished trumpeters are giant fifty-foot-tall angels and not mere puny Israelite mortals:* He shall see that their hand is weakened with *no jacks or better pairs,* and that they who were shut-up have also failed *and will not be able to speak any more irresponsible bullshit,* and they that remained are consumed *for the Lord's just desserts.*

See ye that I alone am, and there is no other God besides Me *or beside Me' either:* I will kill and I will make to live, *for I have the supernatural prerogative to do either thing or do anything involving life and death decisions, all at My leisurely discretion.* I will strike, *and perhaps even refuse to work in My' spare time,* and I will heal, *but not obey humans like* a *dog;* and there is none that can deliver out of my *superior* hand *of Ace, King, Queen, Jack and Ten, all in potent diamonds!*

If I shall whet my sword as the lightning *does, but not like the senile judges do with their pungent-smelling urine, the awful ancients and the loony priests wet their pants and also their undependable diapers,* and surely, my *superior trumping* hand take hold on My *making final call* judgment: I will render vengeance to my *avowed* enemies, and repay them *in spades, all* the *feckless* idiots that *foolishly* hate Me.

I *(Moses)* will make my *alcoholic* arrows drunk with blood, and my *starving* sword shall *systematically* devour flesh, of the blood of the slain and of the captivity, of the bare head of the Lord's *already bald* foes. *I'll even pilfer the enemy's enemas when necessary.*

I *(about-to-die Moses)* say, "Praise His inferior people *who all need many self-esteem lessons badly,* ye *sinning pagan* nations, for He will revenge the *Type-O negative* blood of His *gay HIV/AIDS* servants: and will render vengeance to their *infected promiscuous gay* enemies *too,* and He will be merciful to His *few loyal* people *who still stubbornly engage in acceptable straight post-marital sex.*

So Moses *(me)* came and spoke all the words of this *disheveled* canticle in the *deaf* ears of the *unreceptive* people, and *also to* Josue, the son of Nun *and the bisexual Pedophile Priest.* And he *(Josue)* ended all these words, speaking to all Israel *without even a rudimentary megaphone or a functional perfunctory artificial voice box.*

And he *(Josue)* said to them *(the mercurial unstable Israelite listeners):* "Set your hearts on all the words, *and I think you'll be all set like the daily sun! Thank you Moses! I'm learning this prophet role routine quite well already! Truer words were never spoken Moses, that is, except those truths and Commandments spoken by the Lord, but in one theatrical process, I'll pretend to accept them!"*

And the *all-too-busy* Lord spoke to Moses *(me)* the same day, saying: "*Even though you're dying,* go up into this mountain Abarim, *(that is to say, of secret shortcut passages)* unto Mount Nebo, which is in the land of Moab *Dickie* over against Jericho: and *from there* see the *anticipated* land of Canaan, which I will deliver to the children of Israel to *proudly* possess, and die thoust in the mountain *Moses because that is where I wish you to expire, just like Angel Gabriel's overdrawn credit card has been recently terminated.* As Aaron thy *incompetent* brother had died in Mount Hor, *being attended to and serviced by a dozen sensuous harlots that never wanted to be paid overtime, and if you recall My' dear Moses, Aaron was buried by the prophet Hank, also known as Hank of Hair.*"

Chapter Thirty-three

"Blessing upon the Tribes"

Moses before his *prescribed* death blesseth the tribes of Israel. This is the blessing, wherewith the man of God, Moses, blessed the *deviate* children of Israel, *while existing in a semi-coma* before his *scheduled* death. And he said *mumbling his words:* "The Lord came from Sinai, *where we Israelites all had severe sinus infections that have lasted us almost forty years,* and from Seir, He rose up to us: He hath appeared from Mount Pharan, and with Him thousands of saints, *accompanied by sundry wandering spirits that were still looking for non-existent admission tickets into Heaven.* In his right hand a fiery law, *whose wild flames made aged Moses experience severe first degree burns on his right hand, fingers wrist and elbow. But it didn't matter, since beloved Moses was already dead!*

According to Josue's declaration and recollection, he *(Moses on his death bed having severe hallucinations)* hath loved the people, and all the *miniaturized* saints *that came marching in and who are now skittering about* in his *(Moses) swollen* hand: and they that approach to his 'feet', *a queer assemblage of miscellaneous fantasized ghosts and ghouls who* shall receive of his (either the Lord's or Moses') doctrine *by reading the Ten Commandment's law and the related nonsensical canticle footnotes.*

Moses commanded us *(me Josue and the gang)* on his death bed a law, the inheritance of the multitude of Jacob, *whose saintly spirit was still flying around as an eagle searching for fabled Philadelphia.* He *(Jacob's lost spirit)* shall be king with the most *correct answers meritoriously attained on the very difficult Biblical Old Testament SAT exam',* the *purple rain* princes of the *recalcitrant* people, being assembled with *and among* the *potentially volatile addled* tribes of Israel.

"Let Reuben live, and not die, and be he small in number. *And allow Reuben to diversify from his delicious sandwiches and begin making and selling tasty hot dogs, just like Brother Nathan does. And conversely, Brother Nathan can bypass Reuben's food monopoly and use Reuben's secret sandwich ingredients' formula without violating the sandwich king's Bible patent."* But Brother Moses cares not *about this picayune shit because the hoary profit has successfully journeyed off to his distant grave.*

This is the blessing of Juda *as once explained by Moses.* "Hear, O Lord, the voice of Juda, and bring him in unto his people: *his hands shall not fight for him, because the rest of his body is also permanently paralyzed.* And Juda shall be *Nathan's hamburger helper* against his *inherited* enemies, *all except Reuben.*"

To Levi also he *(Moses)* had said: *"Levi, you did a great job constructing the beautiful new blue denim canvas tabernacle. Now then, in relation* to thy *lacking* perfection, and *also* thy doctrine be to thy *appointed anointed* holy man, whom thou hast proved in the temptation, and judged at the *addictive* waters of contradiction. *Somebody please tell me what the fuck I just meant to say in plain Yiddish! If so, that lucky person can win two free admissions to our planned new waterpark and amusement center in downtown Godville, namely, BibleWood Great Adventure.*"

"Holy man Aaron," Moses said, who somehow has miraculously come back to life, "although dear Aaron you're usually out there in left field, Hank and you are gonna' hit this Old Testament Deuteronomy Bible thing over the fence and right outa' the fuckin' stadium!"

"Who hath said to his father, and to his mother," *declared Moses on his death bed.* "I do not know you; and to his brethren: I know you not: and their own children they have not known; *these disoriented shallow-minded assholes, all of whom have never been to China, all of whom might have amnesia and all of whom might actually require professional medical treatment, and not inflexible didactical Biblical therapy.* Those others *(the faithful acolytes)* that have kept the law's word, and observed the covenant inscribed on the two tablets, *Moses indicated,* but have not heeded their meaning *or practiced their morality, should register in the next general election as Liberal Pagans.*"

And to Benjamin and his tribe he *(Moses)* said: "The best beloved of the Lord shall dwell confidently in you, *but honestly Benjamin, I don't know how the hell you're gonna' fit all those confident people inside your frail body:* as in a bride chamber shall

200

he abide all the day long, and between his shoulders shall be rest, *so my best advice to you dear Benjamin is to let your naked bride's knees sit upon your shoulders and let your mouth do the rest. Forget having delightful sexual intercourse on your fuckin' honeymoon night!"*

To Joseph *and his tribe* also he *(Moses)* said: "Of the blessing of the Lord be his land, of the fruits of Heaven, *and I guarantee you Joseph that there shall be no gay fruits in the tyrannical Lord's Heaven, if Heaven ever opens for business like BibleWood Great Adventure may in the future over in Godville, once Godville starts being constructed."*

"Ephraim," *claimed Moses upon his death bed,* "your beauty is as of the firstling of a bullock, his horns as the horns of a rhinoceros *exiting horny coming-of-age puberty:* with them shall you help push the nations even to the ends of the Earth *and right into the* major oceans, *which we know don't really exist on any honestly drawn local or world map, and furthermore beloved Ephraim, the oceans are in truth all fictional seas occasionally mentioned in legendary phony Greek mythology folk tales.* These are the multitudes of Ephraim and these' the thousands of Manasses, *all the clan as slow as molasses in January but faster than maple syrup in July."*

And to Zabulon he *(Moses)* said *upon his death bed:* "Rejoice, O Zabulon, remember me in thy going out; *and your friends Isachar and Isachar-burning are both now sleeping inside the giant canvas denim tabernacle. There is no doubt in my pin-headed ancient mind that you and your exciting band Led Zebulon will be the first ones to climb the much-anticipated Stairway to Heaven, that is, once Heaven opens-up for business, right after BibleWood Great Adventure is built inside yet-to-be-planned Godville. I understand that BibleWood will even have an extraordinary Edifice Wrecks Museum erected on the premises. I had learned all about this planned Stairway to Heaven not from Led Zebulon, but from the local arrow smith!"*

At that pregnant moment, Moses had a major kidney failure crisis and the dying sage farted out a large quantity of methane gas from his minuscule withered penis, and then all who were present detected a weak urine trickle being slowly pissed-out of his shrinking asshole. Then the encumbered prophet continued his informative commentary

201

and embellished, "They *(whoever)* shall call the people to the mountain: there shall they sacrifice the victims of justice, *all one million of them (you dumb-fuck asshole Israelites).* Who shall suck as milk the abundance of the sea, and the hidden treasures of the sands? *I'll tell you who! It'll be all those Hebrew suckers; the same ones that P.T. Abraham had been telling me about!"*

And to Gad he *(Moses)* said: "*Egad Gad!* Blessed be you in His breadth *and* in *His breath, but watch out, for you don't want to be exhaled and propelled-out from the Lord's two mighty lungs. Quite candidly, it's much safer to be expelled from the fiery blazing belly' of an infuriated dragon'.* Now then Gad, he hath rested as a lion, and hath seized upon the arm and the top of the head, *so whatever you do Gad, don't let anyone (even a tiger cub) ever attempt to lionize you! Yes Gad, always be humble, or else the all-encompassing sin of pride will make you live in one of the Lord's monstrous lungs until you are speedily expelled as lethal sulfuric volcanic breath during a very deep and exaggerated Divine Exhale! And Gad, kindly tell Egad all about this relevant bullshit that I'm hallucinating and describing. That obnoxious deaf guy could definitely use the sound advice!"*

To Dan, also he *(Moses)* said: "*Dandy* Dan is a young lion, *in fact a dandy lion,* and he shall flow plentifully from Basan *Basin, also known as Basin Basan. Maybe in a few years dear Dan, you can get together with Ube and buy a European river, conduct fantastic boat tours, and be the Lord's first out-of-Israel missionary who will teach barbarians and pagans alike that only married women are to be screwed, but solely in the classic missionary position! And Dan, you and Ube can get into the flow of things on the lengthy river, but if your boat overturns, you'll both have to get out of the flow of things and get into the swim of things. By all means, check your head's circumference and know your cap size!"*

To Aser also he *(Moses)* said: "Let Aser be blessed with children; let him be acceptable to his brethren, and let him dip his foot in oil. *Now Aser, I strongly suggest that you ought to get into the cremation business with your pals Asher, Isachar, and Isachar-burning. With a catchy motto sounding something like 'Ashes to ashes, dust to dust!' you'll never go wrong, and certainly inexpensive cremation is much better than having to put dead people on lay-a-way, and then have to wait months, maybe even years, to be partially paid for your reasonable services!"*

202

Now Israelites, before I go to ascend yonder mountain to gaze *at the gays and the LBGT community* in the soon-to-be-invaded and conquered Promised Land, I humbly wish that Israel shall dwell in *protective* safety, and exist alone *far away from pagans, from heathens, from gentle gentiles, from lesbians, from homos', from marginalized trans-gender transvestites, and especially far away from radicalized M.F. widows.*

And in the final analysis my fellow Hebrews, the hawk eye of Jacob now sees a land of shriveled corn and a field of vinegar-flavored wine, and on the eve of my historic death, the Heavens shall be misty with sweet honey dew. "Holy shit Israelites! I think I see your father Jacob now, flying as a soaring eagle on the eastern horizon, yes, adroitly zooming over the soon-to-be-vanquished Promised Land, heading in the general direction of Philadelphia!"

"Goodbye and farewell idiot Israelites! Goodbye beloved Israel! Good riddance to you both! I can't wait to see the Promised Land from yonder mountain top and then finally fuckin' die. It's now your fucked-up baby Josue! It's now all your fuckin' baby!"

Chapter Thirty-four

"Death and Burial of Moses"

Moses seeth the Promised Land from the adjacent mountain peak, but is not suffered to go into it *because even the sometimes sadistic Lord had realized that the ancient prophet had already suffered enough during his lengthy tenure upon this Earth.* He dieth at the age of 120 years, *four months, eight days, six hours, seven minutes and three and a half seconds, and upon hearing the propitious news, all million Israelites assembled in the neighboring desert valley boisterously cheered and celebrated for forty consecutive days and forty nights non-stop until a violent earthquake and a gigantic volcanic eruption finally shut the exuberant rabble up.*

God burieth his body *(Moses, not the Lord)* secretly, *not trusting any Israelite morticians, undertakers, funeral directors, cemetery caretakers, the militant grave-diggers union, Jacob the dead flying eagle, embalmers, cremators, or either experienced Asher or veteran Isachar or Isachar-burning to perform the required task.*

Josue, being replenished by imposition of Moses's hands *performing oddball semaphores from the adjacent mountain peak right before the aged prophet imploded in a mystical-but-spectacular pre-historic chemical reaction. Now with the rather predictable-but-unpredictable* spirit of God succeedeth, *Josue then eulogized his eminent predecessor to a now-receptive small audience consisting primarily of the three loyal yellow-stained-diaper ancients, who politely pissed and applauded intermittently throughout Josue's impromptu oration.* Moses, for his special familiarity with God, and for his most wonderful miracles, was commended above all other Hebrew prophets, *the honored group including the predatory dead flying eagle Jacob, who was frenetically hovering above Death Valley (Valley of Death).*

Then after Moses *had died and instantaneously disintegrated into a pile of dust, the revered prophet's spirit* went-up from the plains of Moab *Dickie* upon Mount Nebo, to the top of Phasga over against *yonder* Jericho: and the Lord showed him *(Moses's ghost)* all the land of Galaad as far as Dan, *but since Moses was now happily*

205

dead, he just didn't give a Jacob flying shit anymore about anything happening down on Earth.

And all Nephtali, and the land of Ephraim and Manasses, *flowing with rivers of goat's milk, pure honey and gooey molasses,* and all the land of Juda unto the furthermost *no-name gigantic anonymous western* sea.

And the *lower* south part *of the geography,* and the breadth of the plain of Jericho, the city of majestic palm trees as far as Segor *and affiliated Igor.* And the *Almighty* Lord said to him *(Moses's now-apathetic nomadic ghost):* "This is the land, for which I swore to Abraham and Isaac saying: 'I will give it to thy seed *instead of to your mangy mutt.* Thou hast seen it with thy *own* eyes, and shalt not pass over to it *until Jacob stops being a show-off fly-by-night eagle trying to find Philadelphia'.*"

And Moses, *now* the *ghost (spiritual)* servant of the Lord, had died there, in the land of Moab *Dickie,* by the *arbitrary* Commandment of the Lord, *executed by means of the eagle Jacob bombing decrepit Moses with heavy duty soft bird crap, thus triggering a tremendous chemical reaction-type explosion that immediately incinerated into ashes the revered prophet's dead body.*

Moses *had* died there *in a tremendous prehistoric explosion.* And this *comprehensive* last chapter of Deuteronomy, in which the death of Moses is related, was written *over a forty year period* by Josue, or perhaps by *some of the more grammatically skilled and more rational politically correct* other *demented* prophets *of the day.*

And He *(the Lord supervising Michael and Gabriel collecting remaining body fragments)* buried him *(the tiny remnant pieces left of Moses)* in the valley of the land of Moab *Dickie, where Moses as a young man had a whale of a time partying with the then young bladder-controlled ancients, which is located* over against Phogor: and no man hath known of his *(Moses)* sepulcher until this present day, *not even Moses's 3,650 year old anonymous girlfriend. The Lord wanted the secret tomb to remain unknown out of fear that the idol worshiping Israelites might start adoring the dead Moses and not the always-vindictive living Lord.*

206

He *(the jealous Lord) and His subordinate* archangels would have the place of his *(Moses)* burial to be unknown, lest the *unstable* Israelites, who were prone to idolatry, *might succumb to temptation and* visit the shrine *and start idolizing and praising the sage prophet and not pay obligatory homage to the Almighty Lord.*

And Josue, the son of Nun *and the senile Pedophile Priest,* was filled with the spirit of wisdom, because Moses had laid his hands upon him and had beaten *the trapped crap out of* him, *all from his (locked out of Heaven) dead spirit state.* And the children of Israel obeyed him *(Josue) for a full week,* and did as the Lord commanded Moses *with the plethora of wholly debatable covenants for seven monotonous boring days.*

And there arose no more a prophet in Israel like unto Moses, whom the Lord *truly* knew face to face, *cheek to cheek.* In all the *non-zodiac* signs and wonders, which He *(the surreptitious Lord)* sent by him *(the equally surreptitious Moses),* to do in the land of Egypt to the *victimized anonymous* Pharaoh, and to all his *equally victimized ministers and* servants, and to his whole *victimized* land, *the Lord's mathematical equation was finally balanced with both terrified sides being equal.*

And all the mighty hand *accomplishments,* and *all* the great *Biblical* miracles, which Moses *skillfully* performed before all Israel, *are thoroughly and comprehensively described in the Wholly Book of Genesis, in the Wholly Book of Exodus and finally, in the Wholly Book of Doo-Doo-Rot-on-Me.*

About the Author's Books

Jay Dubya is author John Wiessner's pen name and also his initials (J.W.) John is a retired New Jersey public school English teacher and he had taught the subject for thirty-four years. John lives in southern New Jersey with wife Joanne and the couple has three grown sons. John is the creator of forty-seven hardcover/paperback books.

Jay Dubya has written adult satires Fractured Frazzled Folk Fables and Fairy Farces and FFFF and FF, Part II. Black Leather and Blue Denim, A '50s Novel and its sequel, The Great Teen Fruit War, A 1960' Novel and Frat' Brats, A '60s Novel are adult-oriented literary endeavors constituting a trilogy.

Pieces of Eight, Pieces of Eight, Part II, Pieces of Eight Part III and Pieces of Eight, Part IV are' short story/novella collections featuring science fiction, paranormal and humorous plots and themes. Nine New Novellas is the companion book to Nine New Novellas, Part II, Nine New Novellas, Part III and Nine New Novellas, Part IV. And So Ya' Wanna' Be A Teacher is a satirical autobiography describing the author's thirty-four year educational career in American public schools.

Ron Coyote, Man of La Mangia is adult humor and the work is an imaginative satire/parody on Miguel Cervantes' Don Quixote, published in 1605. Mauled Maimed Mangled Mutilated Mythology is a work that satires twenty-one famous ancient tales. The Wholly Book of Genesis and The Wholly Book of Exodus are also adult satirical humor. Thirteen Sick Tasteless Classics, Thirteen Sick Tasteless Classics, Part II, Thirteen Sick Tasteless Classics, Part III and Thirteen Sick Tasteless Classics, Part IV are adult satirical rewrites of famous short fiction.

John has also authored a trilogy of young adult fantasy novels, Enchanta, Pot of Gold and Space Bugs, Earth Invasion. The Eighteen' Story Gingerbread House is a new collection of eighteen diverse and creative children's stories.

Jay Dubya likes '50s rock and roll music and he also enjoys pop' songs by the Beach Boys', Fleetwood Mac, the Eagles, the Rolling Stones, ELO, John Mellencamp and by John Fogerty.

Author Biography

Born in Hammonton, NJ in 1942, John Wiessner had attended St. Joseph School up to and including Grade 5. After his family moved from Hammonton to Levittown, Pa in 1954, John attended St. Mark School in Bristol, Pa. for Grade 6, St. Michael the Archangel School in Levittown for Grades 7 and 8 and then Immaculate Conception School, Levittown, Pa. for Grade 9. Bishop Egan High School, Levittown Pa was John's educational base for Grades 10 and 11, and later in 1960, the aspiring author graduated from Edgewood Regional High, Tansboro, NJ. John then next attended Glassboro State College, where he was an announcer for the school's baseball games and also read the nightly news and sports over WGLS, GSC's radio station.

John Wiessner had been primarily an English teacher in the Hammonton Public School System for 34 years, specializing in the instruction of middle school language arts. Mr. Wiessner was quite active in the Hammonton Education Association, serving in the capacities of Vice-President, building representative and finally, teachers' head negotiator for 7 years. During his lengthy teaching career, John had been nominated into "Who's Who Among American Teachers" three times. He also was quite active giving professional workshops at schools around South Jersey on the subjects of creative writing and the use of movie videos to motivate students to organize their classroom theme compositions.

John Wiessner was very active in community service, being a past President of the Hammonton Lions Club, where he also functioned for many years as the club's Tail-Twister, Vice-President and Liontamer. John had been named Hammonton Lion of the Year in 1979 and in 2009 received the prestigious Melvin Jones Fellow Award, the highest honor a Lion can receive from Lions International.

John also was a successful businessman, starting with being a Philadelphia Bulletin newspaper delivery boy for two years in the late 1950s in Levittown, Pennsylvania. After his family moved back to New Jersey in 1959, John worked at his grandparents and his parents' farm markets, Square Deal Farm (now Ron's Gardens in Hammonton) and Pete's Farm Market in Elm, respectively. He later managed his wife's parents' farm market, White Horse Farms in Elm for three summers.

Also in a business capacity, for 16 summers starting in 1967 John Wiessner had co-owned Dealers Choice Amusement Arcade on the

Ocean City, Maryland boardwalk and also co-owned the New Horizon Tee-Shirt Store for eight summers (1973-'81) on the Rehoboth Beach, Delaware boardwalk. In addition, "Jay Dubya" was a co-owner of Wheel and Deal Amusement Arcade, Missouri Avenue and Boardwalk, Atlantic City. And then, for 18 summers beginning in 1986, John had been the Field Manager in charge of crew-leaders for Atlantic Blueberry Company (the world's largest cultivated blueberry farm), both the Weymouth and Mays Landing Divisions.

After retiring from teaching in 1999, writing under the pen name Jay Dubya (his initials), John Wiessner became the author of 47 books in the genre Action/Adventure Novels, Sci-Fi/Paranormal Story Collections, Adult Satire, Young Adult Fantasy Novels and Non-Fiction Books. His books exist in hardcover, in paperback and in popular Kindle and Nook e-book formats.

CPSIA information can be obtained at www.ICGtesting.com
Printed in the USA
BVOW02*2355230615

405876BV00005B/39/P